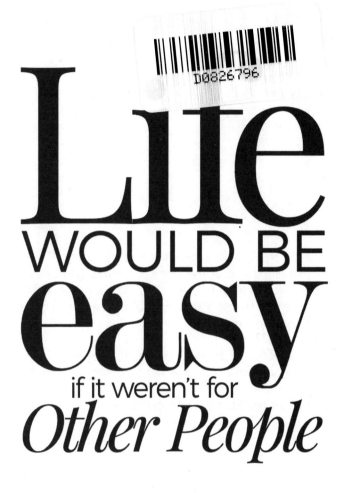

Life
WOULD BE
easy
if it weren't for
Other People

CONNIE PODESTA

STANDOUT PRESS
Dallas, Texas

First edition published 1999
Second edition published 2010
Third edition published 2017

Published by:
STANDOUT Press
18208 Preston Road; Suite D-9
Dallas, Texas 75252
(972) 596-5501

The strategies that follow are not intended to provide guidance in dealing with people who are dangerous or mentally unstable.

Printed in the United States of America.

Editor/Content Development: Susan Priddy (www.SusanPriddy.com)
Design for Cover/Interior: Kendra Cagle (www.5LakesDesign.com)

Library of Congress Control Number: 2017904977

ISBN: 978-1-946225-06-1 (paperback)
           978-1-946225-07-8 (Kindle)
           978-1-946225-08-5 (ePub)

Connie Podesta Presents, LLC
connie@conniepodesta.com
www.conniepodesta.com

DEDICATION

————————

To those who are struggling to work with, lead, report to,
sell to, associate with, parent, and live with difficult people...

This book is dedicated to you.

WELCOME TO THE EXCITING, ALL-NEW
BUSINESS VERSION
OF MY BEST-SELLER!

When I first published this book in 1999, the content was focused mostly on personal relationships.

THIS EDITION IS VASTLY DIFFERENT.

I've spent the past two decades sharing my expertise in leadership, sales, and communication with people in the world's top companies. I have coached, counseled, and interviewed professionals at all levels of every industry. These experiences have totally changed the dynamics of this book.

Instead of providing guidance that is predominantly designed for families and couples, this version is a goldmine of killer work strategies. I've transformed my perennial best-seller into a bold, targeted operating manual for your professional *and* personal relationships.

The four communication styles that drive all of our interactions still form the foundation for the book, but the focus is completely different. It's a much deeper dive. A fresh approach. A brand-new attitude with an edgy business perspective.

Here's to your success!

Connie

The strategies that follow are not intended to provide guidance in dealing with people who are dangerous or mentally unstable.

If you find yourself in a relationship with someone who is physically abusive or emotionally disturbed, get help. Never avoid or ignore threats. Remove yourself from harm's way immediately, and then seek the protection and support you need. Don't wait.

TABLE OF CONTENTS

———————

Caution:
RELATIONSHIPS AT RISK

––––––––––––

No sugar-coating here. Are there people in your life who drive you absolutely out of your mind? I'm talking stark-raving mad. You know, the ones who always seem to leave you banging your head against the wall in frustration.

"Oh, I most definitely know them...not enough stress relief exercises on the planet to combat that kind of crazy."

Well, then you're in the right place. This is the book for YOU!

LET'S FACE IT:

Most of us have to interact and communicate with people who aren't the easiest to be around. We work with them. Lead them. Report to them. Sell to them. Partner with them. Even live with them.

During my 30 years of coaching, counseling, interviewing, and speaking to more than two million people worldwide, I have learned a fact that appears to be universal and timeless:

1

> **Much of the stress we experience in life stems from the irritating, anxiety-driven, energy-sapping, joy-killing, guilt-producing, and even contentious relationships we have with other people.**

"Nailed it! Relationships can be really stressful."

That explains why this book has always been my best-seller; it's also my most requested speaking presentation.

To be clear, I'm not talking about the one-time encounter with a difficult person in a rush-hour traffic jam, busy grocery store line, or car-servicing center. Isolated confrontations with strangers just happen occasionally. In those instances, my advice is to use any short-term strategies available to extricate yourself as soon as possible with your dignity (or life) intact.

Instead, I will be discussing the people you really can't avoid (without changing jobs or moving to another state): your co-workers, team members, managers, customers, significant others, children, teenagers, and friends.

I'm focusing on the people with whom you have ongoing, up-close-and-personal relationships that impact your life on a regular basis. Probably every day. Sometimes nonstop. Which is exactly why their annoying habits and personality "quirks" prompt an immediate spike in your blood pressure and threaten to send you right over the edge. Head first. Screaming the whole way.

"Lots and lots of screaming. And feeling hopelessly stuck."

You're visualizing one or more of those people right now, aren't you?

OK, deep breath.

If you can relate to this, you're in good company. We ALL have to deal with difficult people in our lives.

"But seriously...I have read enough books on difficult people!"

Not like this.

Most resources offer the reader fascinating techniques to use when interacting with those who have challenging personalities. But, frankly, that's not enough.

Those strategies might deliver a "quick fix," but they won't measurably improve communications and establish healthier, long-term relationships. To be successful, the person using the strategies needs to have insights into the psychological aspects of human behavior.

"That sounds intense...I'm pretty busy."

I'm sure you are. Welcome to our crazy, insane, Internet-driven, 24/7 world. But think about it. A HUGE portion of your "busy-ness" is spent dealing with a few people who are literally sucking the energy out of your body, brain, heart, and soul.

Emotionally and physically, stress is deadly. Which means difficult people are robbing you of your peace *and* your health.

NOT TO MENTION...

- Destroying your last bit of sanity
- Raising your blood pressure
- Lowering your immune system
- Increasing insomnia
- Contributing to weight gain
- Causing your confidence to plummet
- Creating more havoc in your life than you ever thought possible

Just imagine how much more you could accomplish if you spent far less time dealing with the crazy-makers and more time...

- Doing your job
- Mentoring your team
- Increasing your skills
- Leading more effectively
- Closing more deals
- Earning more money
- Sharing time with your partner
- Creating great memories with your kids
- Planning your future

My advice?

Take the extra time to figure people out. Understand what makes them tick, and learn about yourself while you're at it.

> # No matter how long it takes to read this book and learn these lessons, I am saving you tons of hours, money, and sanity in the long run.

Cool, huh?

"Definitely. So what's the catch?"

No catch. Just strategies that get real results **OVER TIME.**

This book is definitely not a quick fix. I know that's what everyone is looking for. But unfortunately, most quick fixes are scams anyway. You know the ones: *"Earn $100K in 4 weeks!" or "Lose 20 pounds in 5 days!"*

It's just not logical. Difficult relationships don't appear overnight. They develop and deteriorate over time, so correcting them isn't an overnight project.

Just as maintaining a healthy lifestyle requires a sustained commitment, so does the process of developing and maintaining healthy relationships and communication patterns. Focusing on long-term solutions is far more beneficial than a short-term bandage. Trust me on this.

"Got it. It's a marathon, not a sprint. What's first?"

Begin with a willingness to look at yourself on a deeper level and answer some tough, personal questions. I'm talking about brutal honesty. Truly knowing yourself is, indeed, a game changer. Start here:

- What drives the way you act and react to other people?
- How do you choose to communicate in most situations?
- What attitudes and behaviors are you willing to adjust that may, in turn, change the way other people treat you and communicate with you?
- What role do you play in your most frustrating relationships, both personal and professional?

"Hold on...I thought this book was about other people. Not me."

Glad you brought that up. I hate to break it to you, but we actually DO play a role in those prickly relationships that drive us nuts.

Yes, it's critical for us to understand the people we label as "difficult." We need to learn how to communicate with them, manage them, and respond to them. But relationships are formed by two people, and we have to look at both sides of the equation to determine what's not adding up.

That's the unique difference in my process—and the challenge. If you're as committed to learning about yourself as you are to learning about other people, this book can change your life.

With that said, let's make sure we're on the same page. I am NOT saying that your difficult relationships are your fault. And I'm definitely not trying to convince you that the world isn't filled with its fair share of rude, insensitive, whiny, apathetic, and manipulative people. On the contrary. There's no shortage of individuals who can make our lives miserable.

BUT HERE'S THE GOOD NEWS:

Taking action to analyze yourself and your relationships will put you back in control.

How awesome would that be?

You'll begin to understand what motivates these people. Why they act and react the way they do. What "payoff" they are seeking. How you may play a part in the dysfunctional dance. You might even discover (gasp!) that some of the techniques you are using to deter their behaviors are actually making them worse.

Do you really want to allow these people to continue driving you batty? Or do you want to do something about it? This book will guide you through the process, step by step.

"Now you have my attention."

It's a real eye-opener, right?

Before we move forward, there's one more awkward order of business. We must all be willing to admit one thing:

At some point in our lives, WE have been the difficult person who drove someone else crazy.

An uncomfortable thought, but I guarantee it's the absolute truth.

Humbling, isn't it? Yet somehow it evens the playing field. We ALL struggle with relationships in some area, whether that's at work or at home. Thankfully, the strategies in this book will benefit every part of your life. Professional. Personal. And everywhere in between.

"Count me in. Now what?"

It's time to begin a fascinating journey through the minds of the people who are making you completely bonkers. Plus, I'm throwing in an insightful tour of your own thought processes at no charge. The destination? A beautiful place where you can live your life in control—without letting the frantic, crazy, irritating people take over.

No, you can't find it on TripAdvisor. But I guarantee it's a place you'll never, ever want to leave.

You'll learn more about those people who flat-out annoy the heck out of you. You'll gain insights about yourself. And you'll discover hidden strategies to build stronger relationships, elevate your career, and achieve greater success in everything you do.

My goal is to help you regain control in your life. Ready for that? It's a choice. YOU have the choice, and you have the power to make a change.

Settle in. Keep reading. And prepare yourself for a world with much less stress—and far more peace and happiness.

I bet you are ready for some of that, right?

{
REALITY CHECK

Difficult people stealing your sanity?
Stop the crime! You have the power
to take back control!

#stopsanitytheft
}

chapter
one

THE ROOT OF
THE PROBLEM

———————

Let's start by identifying the root of the "difficult people" problem. Deep underground.

Almost all of us are born with the capacity to LOVE and be loved. It's just how we're wired. We have an innate desire to be HAPPY.

We also have the glorious power of CHOICE. We can choose how to act and react to every situation. We can choose to be powerful in our communications. Or powerless.

So, theoretically, the world should be filled with happy people. Because why would anyone choose to be rude, obnoxious, sullen, and apathetic rather than friendly, optimistic, considerate, and supportive?

GOOD QUESTION! NOW FOR SOME REALITY.

We all know people who seem to be avoiding happiness at all costs. They make unwise choices. They have negative attitudes. And then they rationalize their poor behavior and unacceptable actions by saying things like: *"I was just born that way"* or *"It's not my fault; this is who I am."*

Nope. That's not how it works.

"So what happened to change those people?"

To answer that, we must look at the early childhood years when their basic personalities were beginning to take shape.

This is the really sad part about most difficult people. Somewhere along the line, they were "trained" to behave the way they do. In fact, it's even more tragic: they were likely rewarded for their negative actions.

Can you believe that?

Difficult behavior worked for them as children and, more importantly, it continues to work for them as adults.

Here's the backstory. As infants, we thrive on being spoken to, held, and rocked. We respond enthusiastically to the simplest forms of affection—smiles and touch. We learn from those verbal, visual, and physical cues about the principles of cause and effect.

Babies quickly learn how to adjust their behavior to obtain the positive responses they want. They cry or scream if they want to be fed. Or changed. Or held. In other words, they figure out the system.

"Hey, I let out a wail, and someone shows up to get me whatever I need. Awesome!"

As we grow older, we begin to more closely match our behaviors with the responses they generate, and record those reactions in our subconscious. After each action, we evaluate: were my needs met as a result of what I just said or did?

"Interesting. But how do we keep track of all that?"

Just imagine our subconscious minds as internal filing cabinets where information is stored in one of two drawers, *"Positive: Behaviors that Worked"* or *"Negative: Behaviors that Didn't Work."*

As we fill up these drawers, our future adult personalities begin to take shape. We repeat the things that work. We ditch the things that don't (and try something new the next time). It's a process that continues throughout childhood and adolescence.

With every step, we're exploring which actions will prompt our parents, teachers, or friends to give us what we want.

> # In the game of life, the object is to get our needs met.

Once our very basic human needs of food and shelter are taken care of, most of what we say and do revolves around our need to be...

- Loved
- Liked
- Recognized
- Appreciated
- Respected
- Treated Fairly

...by other people whom we view as necessary or important.

The truth is, **we are ALL playing the needs game.** We started learning the rules from the minute we were born and refined them over the early years. We figured out what we had to do to get our needs met—and we kept doing that.

THE RESULT?

A life-long strategy for behavior and communication. Deeply ingrained. Virtually automatic.

An example may be helpful here. Think about children who want cookies before dinner. Some will ask respectfully and use good manners. Others whine, cry, and throw a tantrum. To them, the process is irrelevant as long as it ends with a reward—in this case, cookies.

Whatever behavior produces a cookie is viewed as the winner. Might have been the manners or the manipulation. Doesn't matter. Each child files that information in the appropriate drawer with a note that says, *"Works great! Do it again!"*

Children whose needs were met when they acted lovingly and responsibly tend to continue using positive behaviors as adults. And, of course, those whose needs were met as a result of being nasty, hurtful, pouty, sarcastic, or mean will most likely continue on that path throughout their lives.

But wait. It gets worse.

> **Children who can successfully and repeatedly manipulate adults learn to enjoy the ensuing feelings of power and control that result from their manipulation.**

Unfortunately, those same techniques then become part of their normal relationship strategies as adults. It's like there's a long training program for difficult people, and they can't graduate if they don't make others feel powerless. They are still using the same manipulative tricks they learned during childhood—and the buzz they get from them as grown-ups is every bit as good.

"I've seen that behavior. Too many times."

Then let's change that. Starting now. I'm not suggesting that these people won't still annoy you, but you may begin to view their behavior with fresh insight. You'll recognize that their natural-born need to be loved, liked, and appreciated has become secondary to their need to be in charge. The need to be respected may have been sacrificed for or confused with the need to control others.

If you can generate the tiniest bit of compassion for their needs-driven descent into bad behavior, you may be able to see the difficult people in your life from a new perspective.

"That sounds ambitious at the moment. But what's my role in all of this?"

Well, think of the people in your life who consistently behave toward you in unacceptable ways. Then ask yourself the most important question: could you be *inadvertently* rewarding their negative behavior in some manner?

That's tough for most of us to answer. We rarely view our responses and reactions to inappropriate or even abusive behavior as positive or rewarding. But the key is looking at the situation from the other person's viewpoint. Perhaps what we intended as a deterrent is instead viewed as a reward.

Consider the cause and effect in these inadvertent-reward scenarios.

#1

After staff cutbacks, everyone at the company was working harder than ever. Jason needed assistance with a customer and asked Ryan for help. Even though Ryan wasn't doing anything at the time, he angrily shouted, *"That's not my job!"* right in front of the customer. Jason became flustered and quickly asked another employee to step in. Before long, the word was out. If you need help, don't go to Ryan.

LESSON LEARNED:

To get away with doing the least amount of work, just refuse to cooperate and create an awkward scene. You will continue to be paid, and everyone will leave you alone.

#2

Ashley is a member of your team at work. She repeatedly comes in late. Takes more than her share of sick days. Rarely turns in projects on time. And yet, the team leader refuses to take real action. Ashley has been "warned" and "talked to," but her behavior doesn't change. To make matters worse, you are now asked to work overtime and take on some of her projects because Ashley can't be trusted to do them correctly.

LESSON LEARNED:

Underperforming is rewarded with a paycheck, shorter hours, and less stress. If you do your job well, you will be penalized and forced to pick up the slack for everyone else.

#3

Don loves to play golf on the weekends, but his wife Lisa doesn't like him to be away from home so much. Don regularly picks a fight with Lisa toward the end of the week, arguing about any issue that's convenient. Once she starts sulking and gives Don the silent treatment, he's out the door on Saturday for 18 holes of golf.

LESSON LEARNED:

If your significant other isn't on board with your plans, just initiate a fight that results in the silent treatment as punishment. You'll be free to do whatever you want.

#4

Zach is a teenager living with his mom, who is recently divorced and feeling lonely. After they eat dinner, Zach's mom really wants him to stay downstairs and watch TV with her. Every time Zach tries to tell her that he just wants to go hang out in his room, she gets her feelings hurt. He feels guilty and ends up staying. One night she gave him a hard time about going upstairs to make a phone call to his girlfriend. In frustration, he yells, *"I hate you!"* Zach's mom wanted him to know that behavior was unacceptable, so she immediately sent him to his room.

LESSON LEARNED:

If you want to spend the evening alone, just yell and be disrespectful. Then you will be sent to your room for an evening of peace and quiet.

Starting to make sense? Consequences and punishments often end up delivering the recipients' desired results.

> # We are constantly rewarding others, even though it may not look like it on the surface.

No one is actually handing out trophies for unacceptable behavior, but psychological rewards are seductively compelling. People are wired to do whatever it takes to get their needs met. When they land on something that works, they are enticed and incentivized to repeat those actions. Over and over.

"That's disturbing. But it does shed new light on some of the conflicts at work."

Exactly. I work with companies throughout the world in all industries. Some are large Fortune 500 organizations and others are small, family-owned businesses. Regardless of the location or size, I continually witness the same scene: difficult people constantly getting what they want. Managers inadvertently make accommodations for them in the form of some very attractive benefits.

1. BETTER SCHEDULES

We don't want to make them any more irritable by asking them to stay late or giving them the worst shifts.

2. FEWER PROJECTS

We know difficult people are not the easiest to work with, so we minimize their assignments on teams and committees to avoid complaints.

3. EASIER CUSTOMERS

We simply can't trust them with the high-stakes clients who might need more finesse in terms of problem resolution.

4. LOWER STANDARDS

We avoid unnecessary confrontations with them at all costs, so they turn in projects late and leave early without any ramifications.

5. REDUCED ACCOUNTABILITY

We think it's easier to ignore their attitudes, actions, and mistakes rather than to call them on their behavior and deal with them directly.

What a deal, right? And they continue to collect a paycheck just like everyone else who is trying to be pleasant, cooperative, and conscientious.

> # Difficult people are usually rewarded for their unacceptable and inappropriate behavior, so why should they change?

That's the root of the problem.

We may be responding to difficult people in ways that meet their needs and actually encourage the unacceptable behaviors we want to eliminate. When we refuse to hold them accountable, we are setting the stage for the development of an unhealthy (and perhaps destructive) relationship.

Difficult people gain control. And we allow ourselves to become emotional hostages.

A painful realization, right?

Once that sinks in, go ahead. Let out the primal scream. Then grab a cup of coffee; we've got work to do.

{
REALITY CHECK

Are you unknowingly rewarding the bad behavior of the difficult people in your life?

#selfinflictedwounds
}

SUMMARY
Points to Remember

1. We are all born with the capacity to love and the power to choose our actions.
2. Life is about getting our needs met, and that's an unspoken priority in every relationship.
3. We track what works (and what doesn't) in the quest to get our needs met, and we repeat the behaviors that lead to success.
4. We train other people how to treat us by establishing (or not establishing) boundaries.
5. Sometimes we inadvertently encourage bad behavior by not standing up to others and failing to insist on fair treatment.
6. Certain people enjoy the power and control that comes with manipulation, which leads them to repeatedly mistreat others.
7. When we work with difficult people, we may hold them to lower standards as a way of preventing confrontations.
8. This is the root of the relationship problem: we may be rewarding difficult people for treating us badly.

chapter
two

THE RELATIONSHIP FORMULA

I can imagine what you are thinking right now:

"I am never, ever, ever again going to reward the bad behavior of this person who makes me want to hide under the bed with a Big Gulp and a bag of Cheetos."

Well, maybe that's not exactly what you were thinking, but I'm probably in the right ballpark.

If you want to put a serious stop to this cycle (and I'm guessing that you do), you need to understand the basic framework that's supporting the unwanted chaos.

Let's break it down.

In this chapter, we'll analyze the relationship formula: the powerful, one-two punch of actions and reactions.

We'll begin by taking a 30,000-foot view of the **four communication styles.** The good. The bad. And the painfully frustrating. I'll be discussing each of these in greater depth throughout the book. But for now, this general context will help you begin to identify some of the patterns commonly found among the people who put your sanity and relationships at risk.

Then we'll look at the **four responses or feedback styles** we can select when interacting with others. Some are positive choices; others are not.

Once you can mentally visualize the components of the communication-and-response balancing act, you'll have the tools you need to make positive changes.

Or at least recognize when someone else is seriously messing with you. Knowledge is power, my friends.

"When you talk about communication, are you just referring to actual one-on-one conversations?"

No, it's actually much broader than that. It goes beyond spoken and written words. If you've ever been on the receiving end of "a look that could kill," you understand that words aren't required to transfer a message with perfect clarity. Non-verbal communication, facial expressions, and tone of voice fall into the same category. Even attitudes and behaviors.

Now for the first part of the relationship formula.

In every interaction, we can choose from four basic communication styles:

1. Assertive
2. Aggressive
3. Passive
4. Passive-Aggressive

SPOILER ALERT:

Only the ASSERTIVE communication style will help create, support, and sustain healthy, productive relationships. I'm guessing the difficult people in your life are completely unaware of this approach, but it's going to become your secret weapon. Sweet!

On the next page you'll find a quick list of characteristics associated with each communication style.

Keep in mind, we ALL have used these four communication styles at some point in our lives. Sometimes every one of them within a single day. However, most of us tend to rely on one style far more than the others, which creates the foundation for our dominant personality.

1. When people CHOOSE to use ASSERTIVE COMMUNICATION, they:

- Behave responsibly and respectfully
- Display self-confidence
- Listen carefully with empathy for others
- Lead with influence and a collaborative spirit
- Foster strong, positive relationships
- Get their needs met by clarifying goals and staying focused

2. When people CHOOSE to use AGGRESSIVE COMMUNICATION, they:

- Insist on getting their own way
- Use anger to manipulate others
- Act hurt to make others feel guilty
- Believe problem-solving can only be "I win/You lose"
- Make others feel small so they can feel more important
- Bully and intimidate the people around them
- Try to get their needs met by remaining stubborn and inflexible

3. When people CHOOSE to use PASSIVE COMMUNICATION, they:

- Keep quiet rather than expressing feelings or opinions
- Avoid conflict at all costs
- Allow others' needs to take priority
- Lack self-confidence

- Take a submissive position in most negotiations
- Struggle to make decisions
- Have a difficult time getting their needs met

4. When people CHOOSE to use PASSIVE-AGGRESSIVE COMMUNICATION, they:

- Lack the emotional maturity to deal with issues head-on
- Perceive themselves as victims
- Hold grudges and assign evil intent to words or actions
- Silently manipulate others to get revenge
- Engage in emotional battles to "even the playing field"
- Refuse to acknowledge the silent competition in progress
- Mentally keep score in relationships to get the upper hand
- Try to get their needs met through sabotage and back-stabbing

Are any of those descriptions ringing a bell? Uh-huh. I figured they might.

"So what makes us choose one style over the others?"

The way we decide to communicate is based on our past experiences. We figure out which one works best with certain people and situations, and that becomes our "go-to" choice. More details ahead...

Before we talk about the other half of the equation, we need to get the really frustrating part out of the way. To move from a toxic relationship into a healthy one, you must believe one thing:

> # It is totally impossible to change other people.

I know what you're thinking. THEY are the ones who need to behave differently. Feel differently. Act differently. I get it.

But here's the reality. We can try to understand them. We can react differently to their outbursts or moods. But we absolutely, positively cannot change them. Ever. It simply doesn't work.

Not that we don't try. Every day we see people who are on a mission to change their significant others, children, friends, or parents. What happens? They inevitably end up displaying behaviors that are just as bad. Poor attitudes. Anger. Manipulation. Arrogance. Resentment. They nag, whine, withdraw affection. All in the name of desperately trying to get the other people to change.

BOTTOM LINE: NOT. GOING. TO. HAPPEN.

As long as we are trying to change someone else, we will never be in control of our own emotions, reactions, and well-being. We have to let that go and concentrate on changing what we CAN control.

"And what is that? What CAN I control?"

There's a famous saying that sums up this situation: *we can't change the cards we're dealt, only how we play the hand.* The same principle applies here.

While we can't change other people, we can help them realize it's time to update their psychological filing cabinets. How? We begin RESPONDING to their negative, unacceptable, and inappropriate behaviors in ways that **don't allow them to get their needs met.** Essentially, if we do it right, we can retrain them to treat us differently. Better. Hopefully much better.

Back to the equation.

We can select from four types of responses when we communicate in our relationships.

Every time we respond to someone, we can choose to give them:

1. Positive Feedback
2. Constructive Feedback
3. Destructive Feedback
4. No Feedback

Bonus spoiler alert: only the first two choices will help you successfully change the dynamics of a difficult relationship.

"Great. I need some details."

1. POSITIVE FEEDBACK

When people display appropriate or acceptable behavior that we hope they'll repeat in the future, we should always respond with positive feedback. We need to let them know we recognize and appreciate what they said or did.

This type of response can come in many different forms. Bonuses. Promotions. An increase in salary. Awards. Blue ribbons. An "A" on a test. An email that says "good job." Hugs, smiles, pats on the back. All the things that make people feel loved and validated. By responding with positive feedback, we are prompting people to carefully file that behavior in the mental drawer with a note that says, *"It worked! Do it again."*

2. CONSTRUCTIVE FEEDBACK

When people engage in negative behaviors or attitudes that we do NOT want repeated, we should always respond with constructive feedback. This assertively lets them know that their words or actions are unacceptable, but we communicate that without being mean or manipulative.

This type of response acknowledges the problem, but shifts the focus to positive strategies for making improvements. Yes, things went wrong, but let's figure out how to make sure this doesn't happen again. The "offenders" feel supported rather than attacked. And the behavior gets filed in the drawer for, *"Didn't work so well. Try these options instead!"*

The emphasis here is on learning and collecting alternatives so that the bad behavior is limited to a one-time-only event. When this type of response is used well, it leaves people with a desire to analyze their actions, communicate more effectively, and do better next time.

3. DESTRUCTIVE FEEDBACK

Unfortunately, many people opt for behavioral payback when others act in unacceptable or inappropriate ways. They choose to respond in a manner that feels spiteful, manipulative, angry, humiliating, or punitive. Rather than focus on constructive feedback that could help to resolve the problem, they resort to harsh criticism. Lashing out. Blame. Put-downs. Sarcasm. That's destructive feedback.

The focus here is definitely on the "bad" person rather than the inappropriate actions, with no hint of encouragement for change or discussion of positive alternatives. Clearly, this approach destroys relationships and paves the way for epic power struggles.

Two outcomes are possible. The recipients of this feedback may get openly defensive *("You can't tell me what to do!")* or quietly defensive *("He's going to pay for this...").* In the meantime, the behavior might appear to stop. But IT DOESN'T. Chances are, the people are plotting their revenge—which may include repeating the bad behavior just to prove that they can. *("You think you've seen the worst? Just wait!")*

4. NO FEEDBACK (AVOID/IGNORE)

When people display poor attitudes and behaviors, we have a fourth option for response: ignoring it. No response at all. No feedback—*or so people think.* Don't be fooled by that. The absence of response actually sends a POWERFUL message. Loud and clear. And not in a good way.

Too often people simply want to avoid confrontation and do nothing. Say nothing. Act like they didn't even notice or care about what just happened. But that presents a huge problem. We have to understand the message that sends when we ignore behaviors that we don't want repeated.

The complete lack of feedback is perceived by the subconscious mind in the same way as a positive response. Avoiding is translated as condoning. Accepting. Allowing. Giving permission. And yes, rewarding. You can bet that behavior is getting filed in the drawer labeled, *"Worked great! Do it again."* No one noticed, or no one cared. Go for it!

The irony is painful. Passive avoidance is perceived as active reinforcement. Bummer.

Doesn't seem fair, does it? I understand most people hate conflict, and that makes avoidance seem very appealing. If you're allergic to nuts, you take a hard pass on the PB&J. It's what you do to prevent hives and wheezing. Same situation with the crazy people in your life. Why would you want to subject yourself to a situation that seems virtually guaranteed to create extreme anxiety and three nights of insomnia?

"That's precisely what I was thinking..."

Well, avoidance might seem like a smart strategy for self-preservation, but I'm going to give you the straight story here.

Consistently avoiding and ignoring difficult people is one of the BIGGEST MISTAKES you can make if you seriously want your relationships with them to improve.

Why? Because you are now a partner in the dysfunction.

Unless your safety is at risk with a potentially serious or dangerous confrontation, you have to stand up and change your response if you want to create a different outcome.

And if you do? You will gain the POWER to generate NEW RESULTS.

(It won't make you a Super Hero, but I'm guessing some super power sounds like a great deal right now.)

"So I need to change the formula?"

Exactly. You can change the outcome by changing your style of communication and the way you respond to the difficult people in your life. At least that's the first step.

But keep in mind that difficult people will probably not be enthused about your new strategy to shake things up and hold them accountable for their actions.

Consider the mindset of difficult people.

THEIR GOALS ARE TO:

- Do their own thing
- In their own time
- In their own way
- On their own terms
- Without any interference from us

Oh, yes. In other words, they want EVERYTHING.

And until now, we've been giving it to them. We've likely been making the same move in the relationship game for a very long time. The formula seems set in stone.

We tolerate their antics. Hold back our own opinions to prevent disagreements. Listen to their tales of woe or arrogant bravado. Give in to their choice of strategy or restaurant because it's easier than arguing. Clean up after them. Pick up the slack. Compromise at 90/10 because—hey!—that's better than nothing.

Even worse, we learn to rescue them repeatedly until it seems the natural thing to do. We may learn to lie for them and make excuses for their bad behavior. We may even learn to accept abuse from them (verbal, physical, sexual, or emotional), all while rationalizing that we must be doing something to deserve it and making excuses for their unacceptable behavior.

This pattern of concessions and accommodations has been formed and reinforced over long periods of time. It's now perceived as normal.

> # When you try to change the standard operating procedure for the relationship, you're probably going to get some *significant* pushback.

In their view, you're not just flipping over the apple cart. It will look like you're flipping it over, smashing it with a sledgehammer, and lighting it on fire. You get the picture.

Difficult people are simply not going to welcome your new-found skills of applying more effective responses. It's a virtual guarantee that they will NOT cave in on your first attempt to change the formula. Be aware of that, but don't let it intimidate you. Commit to the change! You DO want this to change, right?

"Oh, yeah. So exactly what will this pushback look like?"

Given that most difficult people have enjoyed a lifetime of being rewarded for behaving badly, they don't have much experience with anything else. In fact, they are easily irritated and disappointed when things don't go their way. They may complain, connive, sulk, or use the silent treatment.

Typical comments might be:

- *"You never had a problem with this before."*
- *"What's wrong with you?"*
- *"We've always done it this way."*
- *"This is just who I am. I can't help it."*
- *"No one else is concerned about this."*

"Hmmmm...have I mentioned I hate conflict?"

Yes, but it will be worth it. Here is a tough-but-oh-so-valuable principle to help understand the part you may be playing in an unhealthy relationship:

> **In most relationships, we are treated exactly the way we allow ourselves to be treated—and that's usually a reflection of how we treat ourselves.**

Whew! That's difficult to think about, let alone absorb and believe. But understanding ourselves is crucial if we want to change unhealthy relationships into sustainable, respectful ones. As always, it starts with US!

If difficult relationships are taking a heavy toll on your life and your career, I hope you are realizing that you deserve better. More honesty. Less manipulation. More happiness. Less stress.

YOU HAVE THE CHOICE TO MAKE A CHANGE.

During my years of professional counseling and coaching, I have found that the power of choice is a huge revelation. My clients are often quick to admit that they are frustrated, saddened, or depressed because they cannot seem to communicate with some of the most important people in their lives. They definitely don't like the way they are being treated, but they are also disappointed in their own behaviors and reactions to that treatment.

Does that resonate with you? If so, this is your lucky day.

You have choices. Change is now within your grasp. You can hold people accountable and stop that vicious cycle. You can take back control.

If you don't like the current results, you can change the relationship formula.

{

REALITY CHECK

Who's controlling your relationship formula?
If things don't add up, change
the balance of power!

#subtractstress

}

SUMMARY
Points to Remember

1. All people have the power to choose how they communicate and respond to others.
2. If we understand the formula for communications, we can uncover options for changing the value of our relationships.
3. There are four communication styles: Assertive, Aggressive, Passive, and Passive-Aggressive.
4. The assertive style is the only one that will lead to healthy relationships and give us the power to transform the difficult ones.
5. We've all used each of these styles at some point in our lives.
6. We can't change other people, but we can retrain them to treat us better.
7. There are four feedback options: Positive, Constructive, Destructive, and Avoiding/Ignoring.
8. Assertive communicators use positive and constructive feedback to successfully deal with difficult people.
9. When we begin changing our communication styles and responses, the difficult people in our lives may push back at first (but usually not forever).
10. We have a choice to make in changing our relationship formulas, and the potential for positive results is extremely high.

chapter
three

THE
ASSERTIVE STYLE

If you're fired up about the idea of regaining control over your difficult relationships, then this is a pivotal chapter for you.

The assertive style contains the hidden code for changing the relationship formula. In case you skipped the previous spoiler alert, here's a summary:

> **Assertive communications are the only way to create, support, and sustain healthy relationships.**

That's the main thing you want to remember; assertiveness is the goal. Now think about the contrast between these two versions of the same story.

Imagine taking a road trip to a beautiful town you read about on a travel website. You plan the best route and pack carefully. You thoroughly enjoy the scenery along the way. Once you arrive at your destination, you feel energized and can't wait to explore the new city.

Now imagine taking the same trip with a passenger—one who constantly asks you to make detours, stop for snacks, and take every exit with a cheesy souvenir shop or a Starbucks with free Wi-Fi. This highly demanding traveler is getting on your last nerve, and it takes all of the energy and patience you have to reach the destination without unleashing your irritation. Once you do arrive, you're too exhausted to go sightseeing.

The first example illustrates life using assertive communications. You set the goal. You define the pace. You enjoy the process.

The second example demonstrates what happens when you let a difficult person take control of your trip. (Or your career. Or your home. Or your life.) It looks like you're behind the wheel, but you're allowing someone else to navigate every turn. Even taking you down paths you don't want to travel.

> **Difficult people really can drive you crazy. And that can completely ruin the way you experience life every day.**

How sad is that?

"No kidding. And I think I might work with that passenger guy..."

Well, the good news is, you've discovered the solution. Assertiveness is the tool that will put you back in charge of the route and keep you moving in the right direction. Once you make the switch, the assertive style is going to be your new best friend.

Let's start by examining the **four primary components** that form the foundation of the assertive communication style:

1. HONESTY

Openly letting others know about your needs, concerns, and feelings without hidden agendas, game-playing, threats, or manipulation.

2. RESPECT

Genuinely recognizing your own value, as well as the value of others, which prompts you to search for win/win solutions.

3. FAIRNESS

Communicating without judgment, prejudice, or discrimination.

4. CONFIDENCE

Being strong enough to deal with difficult issues (without being confrontational), set limits, enforce boundaries, and hold others accountable without backing down.

That's a powerful combination—and it delivers positive results.

ASSERTIVES KNOW HOW TO:

- Display confidence rather than fear
- Persuade rather than coerce
- Engage with openness rather than secrecy
- Hold others accountable rather than giving in
- Negotiate rather than manipulate
- Take responsibility rather than acting like a victim

With all of those qualities, most Assertives inevitably rise to senior positions within organizations. In the interest of full disclosure, many Aggressives also get promoted. That's the unfortunate outcome when no one is assertive enough to hold them accountable for their unacceptable or inappropriate behavior. More than ever, companies need Assertives to guide their organizations and call people out when they aren't demonstrating admirable leadership.

On the home front, Assertives tend to maintain more balanced lives. They take better care of themselves. And those smart choices typically translate into thriving friendships and long-lasting, healthy relationships.

So here's the really strange part. Even though assertive

communication is the most effective style at work and at home, **it's the least used.**

"That's odd. Why?"

Bottom line, many people just don't know exactly how to be assertive. They didn't grow up with assertive role models, so they never learned the skills required to express their needs, interact maturely, seek other viewpoints, engage in meaningful, open-ended dialogue, or build up their confidence.

Instead, they probably witnessed the other three communication styles on many occasions. That could explain why their strategies for problem-solving often involve either initiating conflict or avoiding it, even though neither of those choices will generate the results they want. People watch and imitate. It's not always a good thing, but it's human nature.

If you're struggling with difficult people, you might not have grown up with role models to teach you the assertive skills you need to improve those relationships. Think back to your childhood years. Any clues?

For instance, parents who discovered you and a sibling arguing over a toy may not have taken the time to discuss the finer points of negotiation skills. Instead, they sent each of you to your rooms, where you needed to stay until you could get along.

The question is: how are you supposed to learn the skills you need to get along better with others in a room by yourself?

In the absence of assertive communication, the first instinct is to separate people who are having problems or disagreements. No wonder the divorce rate is so high! At the first sign of conflict, our go-to solution is separation.

When children learn non-assertive styles, they carry them forward as adults. But before you look back and focus on the disappointments and raw deals from years gone by, you don't have to position yourself as a perpetual victim. I'm here to tell you that the past doesn't have to define your future.

"So can I still learn to communicate more assertively if I grew up with non-assertive role models?"

Absolutely. If you make the choice, the commitment, and the conscious effort, you can replace those difficult relationships in your life with positive, healthy ones. You have the power to make the change. Starting this very minute. Using the strategies you are learning right now.

Assertiveness is not about blaming the people in your past who didn't teach you that type of behavior. It's about taking control and being responsible for your choices from this point forward. There is no room for victims in the role of an assertive person.

Just remember that the shift takes time. Assertiveness is the biggest enemy of difficult people. In fact, it's their worst nightmare because it means you have finally figured them out. And more importantly, you are refusing to be swayed by their manipulative attempts.

"Why does the assertive style give me more choices?"

Being assertive is about exploring the options.

> **Difficult people try to coerce us into meeting their demands by fostering the impression that our choices are severely limited or nonexistent.**

Either we do things their way or I suffer dire consequences.

Whiners hope that we'll give in to stop the whining. Same thing for those with bad tempers. They want us to think their anger will be so unpleasant that the smarter move is to give in to their wishes.

That's the advantage of being assertive. It gives you the confidence to insist on entertaining all the options available, not just those offered by the difficult people. In the world of assertive communication, you don't have to react to coercion, force, guilt, whining, or anger. You can confidently analyze the alternatives and make the best choice.

As part of the assertive strategy, you'll need to calmly reiterate that everyone will be held accountable for their responsibilities and actions. No debate. No negotiation. The formula has changed.

"Sounds like Assertives are very deliberate about choosing their words."

For sure! But it's so much more than that. Their assertive words must be backed up by assertive, non-verbal communications. If their body language, facial expressions, and tone of voice aren't sending the same assertive messages, it doesn't work. People can quickly see right through an assertive statement that is nothing more than window dressing.

The visual cues are more obvious, but let's zero in on tone of voice for a moment.

As a graduate student in Psychology and Human Relations, some of my favorite classes focused on the theories of Transactional Analysis. These systems, developed by renowned psychiatrist Eric Berne, are still widely used today to analyze patterns of human interaction.

One of Berne's most famous theories identified three "voices" or tones that people use when communicating:

THE ADULT TONE

Assertive, attentive, straightforward, thoughtful, rational, non-manipulative, non-threatening.

- Body Language: open, receiving
- Words: well-reasoned statements

THE PARENT TONE

Impatient, demanding, patronizing, finger-pointing, blaming, threatening, authoritarian.

- Body Language: exasperated, annoyed
- Words: critical, dictatorial, judgmental

THE CHILD TONE

Hurt, disappointment, pouting, despair, whining, victim, anger, lack of logic.

- Body Language: eye-rolling, heavy sighs, shoulder shrugs, looking away, tantrums
- Words: exaggerations ("never" and "always")

Plenty of examples are coming to mind, aren't they?

The take-away here is to choose the adult tone to support your assertive statements. That's the fastest way to double your credibility when playing the role of a confident, assertive person.

I realize that adopting the adult tone isn't always easy when you're dealing with difficult people. They have created a boat-load of stress in your life. You're likely to have some pent-up, emotional-hostage feelings that are bubbling under the surface.

Resist the urge to let that resentment take over and paint your new assertive word choices with a vengeful tone. It's tempting, I know. But that's veering into the aggressive or passive-aggressive territory. You don't want to go there.

Keep the bigger goal in mind. You are raising the bar and

setting a new standard for the relationship. Diving back into the mud isn't going to do you any good. Stand your ground. Choose assertive words and deliver them with the adult tone. They make a powerful duo.

> **If your tone and body language aren't sending the same message as your words, your assertiveness won't be believable.**

"I'm confused. Should I basically just try to suppress my emotions?"

Definitely not. There's a common misconception that assertive communicators can't express emotions like sadness or anger. Not true at all.

Everyone will feel sad, disappointed, or betrayed at many points in their lives. Assertives just know how to express their feelings using adult tones, open body language, and reasonable words in ways that allow other people to empathize, sympathize, and offer needed support, with no underlying agenda or manipulation. That's the best formula for healthy communication.

"What kind of reaction will I get when I start changing the formula?"

As I mentioned before, things may get worse before they get better when you begin implementing your assertive style. In other words, moving from dysfunctional relationships to successful ones may be a bumpy ride. I can pretty much guarantee you WON'T be hearing this from your difficult person:

"Thank you so much for asserting yourself when I try to manipulate you. You have forced me to reconsider my behavior and learn to be more assertive myself. I'm glad we can now communicate together in a mature and up-front way."

Not a chance. Be prepared for them to fight back.

But remember it's usually a TEMPORARY SETBACK! If you continue giving in, things will NEVER get better. If you do NOTHING, it will definitely get worse. At your expense.

Wait it out! It will be worth it. Your physical health and your emotional well-being are counting on you.

"Patience sounds like a necessity. But I do like the idea of having choices..."

You should! It's amazing.

Choosing an assertive communication style will help you ACT and REACT to whatever life throws your way.

Assertive communications can neutralize the efforts of others who try to manipulate you. They will keep you calm, poised, and fair in dealing with others. They will ensure that you take responsibility for your own actions and hold others accountable for theirs.

It's empowering to have a choice, and it helps your confidence to shine through. Assertive communications can change your relationships. They can change your life.

And there's an added bonus. Remember the people who have never experienced the assertive style? You can begin modeling positive behavior for all of them. Colleagues. Co-workers. Relatives. Friends. Everyone. And since assertiveness is contagious, just imagine the amazing, relationship-boosting ripple effect.

It's a beautiful thing. Drastically reduced stress for you, and a nice contribution to help save the sanity of humankind. Assertive communications make it possible.

"So is assertive behavior essentially the same as professional behavior?"

In many respects, yes. We think of people who are highly professional as being confident and proactive. Assertive communication has those same components.

Non-assertive people might crumble under the stress of problems at work. They start to show signs of anger and bitterness. They develop "an attitude." They might even ignore issues and hope they'll go away.

Assertive people face challenges head-on and aren't afraid of uncertainty. They are flexible and creative.

They actively scan the horizon for new directions with potential.

But being assertive isn't just about having a positive attitude. It's about being proactive. The Assertives do everything in their power to be prepared for whatever happens next. When situations arise that are beyond their control, they can jump into action with confidence.

> ## Assertive, proactive choices have a big payoff.

Assertive professionals can form trusting relationships, productive partnerships, and outstanding teams. Plus, those who consistently use the assertive style in a business setting experience real, measurable results:

- Healthier relationships with co-workers and clients
- Stronger capacity for collaboration
- Enhanced problem-solving abilities
- More effective leadership skills
- Increased job satisfaction
- Higher income levels
- Expanded career potential

"Sounds like that could be quite an asset for leaders."

Definitely. In so many ways!

> # Assertive communication is what differentiates a boss from a leader.

There's a huge difference between choosing to be a boss and choosing to be a leader. Non-assertive bosses rely on their positions or titles for authority. They tell people what to do, issue orders, and demand action. But by minimizing collaboration and teamwork, they reduce innovation and results.

Assertive leaders spend more time supporting their teams. They ask, rather than order. They encourage feedback. And they use communication that is free from abuse, threats, manipulation, or destructive comments. This creates a scenario where people WANT to work together. Develop new, exciting ideas. Sell more. Produce more. Achieve more. And stay competitive.

"Does assertiveness have an impact on employee engagement?"

Absolutely. In my experience working with hundreds of thousands of professionals, I have found that leaders who use the assertive communication style are the most likely to maximize employee engagement. Assertive leaders don't give up control, but rather provide their team members with the knowledge and insights to get involved mentally, physically, and emotionally.

Employees who report to assertive leaders have a much more solid understanding of how their jobs relate to the bigger picture. They are consistently "plugged in." And as a result of that increased **employee engagement**, they can also:

- Maximize their productivity
- Increase their sales
- Lead more effectively
- Improve customer relationships
- Commit fully to the organization's goals
- Work better as a team
- Collaborate more frequently
- Remain resilient in times of adversity
- Support the overall vision
- Enjoy coming to work

"So does assertiveness promote accountability as well? I know that's critical in the workplace today."

Yes. Assertiveness and accountability go hand in hand. You can't have one without the other.

Accountability sets the boundaries for acceptable, appropriate behavior and follows through with praise and recognition for a job well done (or fair consequences for poor performance).

At its deepest level, accountability is about honor and trust. It's about people making commitments, and our promise to hold them to their word.

Without accountability, we can't have healthy relationships. And people end up doing whatever they want, whenever they want. In other words, chaos!

Leaders who are accountable for their own behaviors (and expect their team members to be accountable) are building a foundation of mutual trust. When those employees understand the rules and know they are non-negotiable, real improvements begin to emerge.

Consider the impact of assertive leadership on these attributes alone:

- Attendance
- Punctuality
- Performance
- Commitment
- Innovation
- Empowerment
- Resilience
- Work Ethic

Impressive, huh?

"Very much! Do people tend to use the assertive style more at work rather than at home?"

THEY DO! FOR TWO REASONS:

1. At work, we are often evaluated and compensated based on our ability to cooperate as a team member, so we make a greater effort to communicate in a more

54

professional, assertive manner. *"It will affect my paycheck? Sure, I can be assertive." "People are watching how I handle this situation. I better do it right."*

2. More businesses today are emphasizing assertiveness skills in their professional development training. They know the bottom-line impact of helping employees to be stronger at conflict resolution, mediation, negotiation, team building, shared leadership, and empowerment. A measurable benefit is a powerful incentive.

"That makes sense. But shouldn't those skills transfer over to our personal relationships?"

In a perfect world, that would be the case. Unfortunately, most people treat assertiveness as a limited commodity. We save our best assertive behavior for the office when all eyes are on us, but we tend to run out of steam at the end of a long day. At 5:00, all bets are off. We are likely to treat the people at work with more patience and respect than we do the people we love at home. Sad, isn't it?

We simply feel more comfortable letting our guards down in relationships with family and friends. They interact with us when we're obviously tired, sick, hungry, bored, and angry. Not our best moments, but we chalk it up to "keeping it real."

"I'm cringing, but I know that's right. I'm not always at my best when I'm at home."

You're not alone. Tempers sometimes flare. Manipulation creeps in. Trust erodes. And occasionally we say and do things that are not easily forgiven or forgotten. Such a shame! Our family and friends deserve to engage with our best assertive selves just as much as our colleagues, leaders, and customers do.

They may deserve it, but they don't always get it. Take divorce, for example. Many sources cite lack of communication as a contributing factor in divorce. In reality, those people are usually communicating regularly. And very clearly. They're manipulating, degrading, avoiding, withdrawing attention, using sarcasm, ignoring, and yelling. Exuding contempt with every interaction. It's not the quantity of communications that determines a healthy relationship; it's the quality.

> **The true culprit in divorces is NOT the lack of communication. It is the absence of ASSERTIVE communication.**

Hands down, assertive communication is the best way to boost your "emotional bottom line" and the strength of your personal connections. Marriages. Partnerships. Dates. Friendships. All of those. Just think of the benefits:

- Deeper relationships
- Increased levels of happiness
- Expanded circles of friends
- Greater sense of trust
- More open, truthful communications

"What can parents do to help their children become more assertive?"

For parents, modeling and teaching assertiveness is extremely important. When the adults in the home express their needs and concerns, solve problems together, and participate in decision-making, the children get a front-row seat to watch assertiveness in action. That will dramatically build their self-confidence and their self-esteem.

But if the children aren't allowed or encouraged to communicate their needs, fears, and concerns, they will soon find other ways to get what they want—and that usually involves manipulation.

Non-assertive parents may even unknowingly put road-blocks in their children's journeys to trust their own feelings.

"Mom, I'm tired."
"No, you're not. You just got up from your nap."

"Dad, I'm hungry."
"You can't be. You just ate lunch."

"Mom, I don't want to go to the party."
"Sure you do! You'll have fun."

When children are taught to distrust their own feelings, they learn to disregard internal warning signs that are crucial for keeping them safe. We should all be able to "trust our gut" when approached by a stranger or venturing into an area that looks somewhat sketchy. Assertiveness is what makes that possible.

For adults and children, assertive communications will give them a foundation for strength and the courage to honor the way they really feel.

"So basically, the assertive style is tied directly to our own self-respect."

Most definitely. Only assertive people garner the respect necessary to create healthy relationships. They know how to develop connections with others that will sustain rather than drain. Build up rather than tear down.

Besides, it's the only way to interact and consistently get your needs met.

> **The quality of your relationships mirrors your relationship with yourself. You have to love and respect yourself first. Everyone else will notice and follow.**

Part of developing that self-respect is standing up for yourself. Take action! Do something that makes you feel more confident. Do something that sends the world a big message that you have the right to be treated well. And back it up.

The interesting fact here?

> **For the most part, difficult people only respect those who have the confidence to stand up for themselves and fight for what they deserve.**

Using the assertive style will give you the tools you need to believe in yourself and make sure others do, too.

"Makes sense. But being assertive takes a big commitment—how do I know I'm ready?"

START BY ASKING YOURSELF THESE QUESTIONS:

- Are you tired of manipulative relationships?
- Are you ready to set parameters and boundaries?
- Are you determined to confront behavior you don't want repeated?
- Are you comfortable implementing consequences for poor behavior and performance?
- Are you committed to transforming your relationships?

Tough questions, I know. But you'll need to answer them before you can work on becoming more assertive and dealing with the difficult people around you.

"So are you saying I am entitled to be treated with respect?"

Nope. I'm not saying that at all. Entitled means you believe you are owed respect no matter what you say or how you act. It implies that you are inherently deserving of special attention, privileges, or treatment without any effort on your part. That's not the case. It takes effort, practice, and patience to create strong, healthy, respectful relationships.

> **Respect begins with us.**

If we want to be treated respectfully, we can't be disrespectful to the people around us. Even the extremely annoying ones who make us want to disappear into the witness protection program. Those are precisely the people who need to learn the respect-privilege rule. The only way to teach them is to behave respectfully toward them (which does NOT mean accepting their manipulation or abuse) and believe we have the right to be treated the same way.

So now it's time for more questions. What about your respect rating? Have you earned the privilege?

- Do you treat others with kindness and courtesy?
- Do you give others the benefit of the doubt?
- Can you interact with empathy and compassion?

- Have you allowed manipulation to creep into your communications?
- Have you slipped into the martyr role?
- Have the irritating people in your life prompted you to retaliate?

Respect is a two-way street. If the rude people in your life have been driving right down the middle and running you off the road, it's time to confidently and respectfully reclaim your side of the highway.

"That all sounds good. But what happens if others refuse to treat me with respect?"

It's always a possibility. Some difficult people are so locked into their ways that they would rather dissolve their relationships rather than adjust. They simply may not be willing to join you in elevating the communication to a higher, healthier level.

And what if they do refuse? Do you really want to continue working or living in a situation where people take advantage of you every day? Where you have to compromise your own values at the expense of your health and sanity?

NOT GOOD OPTIONS.

Maybe it's time to ask yourself some pointed questions.
- Do you currently feel valued by this person?
- Do you trust this person?

- Do you feel comfortable and safe expressing your honest thoughts and opinions with this person?
- Does this relationship limit you in any way?
- Can you continue this relationship indefinitely as it stands now?
- How would your life be better if you improve this relationship?
- How would your life change if this relationship was dissolved?
- Are you sincerely dedicated to changing the dynamics of this relationship?

AND THE MOST IMPORTANT QUESTION OF ALL:

- Do you feel good about yourself when you are in their presence?

Please read that last one again. It's the million-dollar question when it comes to relationships.

Complicated answer? I'm sure. But you're the only one who can sort that out. How bad is it? How stressful is it? How harmful is it to your mental and physical health? What's the potential? Is it worth your time and energy to improve the relationship?

I understand it takes courage to put a relationship at risk. Assertive people must be willing to not only risk it, but perhaps end it and push forward toward something more positive.

> ### If it's not worth it, let it go.
> ### If it is worth it, get ready to make a
> ### change in yourself. BIG TIME.

With that said, here's something to keep in mind. Dissolving a relationship without any attempt to communicate or resolve an issue is **avoidance**. You also shouldn't walk away because life isn't fair, things are uncomfortable, work is hard, change is stressful, or you want the easy way out.

That's giving up. And that's NOT the answer.

"So what is the answer?"

Assertiveness! Whether you decide to make improvements and face your tormentor or move on, this communication style will give you the momentum you need to get where you are going.

Assertives take control. They truly value quality of life—and understand that there is life beyond difficult relationships. They've developed a comfortable, supportive relationship with themselves, so they aren't terrified of being alone. They believe in themselves enough to know that they CAN find something better.

"But I don't want to be a quitter."

Here's a truth that might surprise you. Some of the most successful people in the world are great quitters!

THEY'VE QUIT...

- Jobs
- Relationships
- Projects
- Behaviors
- Attitudes
- Ideas
- Strategies
- Mindsets

...all things that consistently DID NOT WORK!

Sometimes being assertive is knowing when it's imperative to disengage for the sake of your own well-being. If you recognize that the lack of respect isn't changing despite your efforts, it's time to take a stand and protect yourself. Get help if you need it. Get out of harm's way. Saying NO to that type of situation isn't selfish; it's smart.

Assertive behavior gives you the courage to insist on the positive communication you deserve. When you respect yourself, assertiveness begins and manipulation ends.

{
REALITY CHECK

Assertives use honesty, respect, fairness, and confidence to win BIG. At work. At home. At life!

#assertiveswin
}

SUMMARY
Points to Remember

1. The assertive communication style is the best solution for dealing with difficult people.
2. The assertive style is based on a foundation of honesty, respect, fairness, and confidence.
3. While the assertive communication style is the most effective one, it is also the least used because many people never learned the required skills.
4. Learning to be assertive involves making a conscious choice, recognizing that we have options, and holding ourselves and others accountable for their actions.
5. Becoming more assertive may initially create more tension with the difficult people in our lives.
6. Eventually most difficult people will begin to react differently to our new assertive stance, as the relationships thrive and grow.
7. Assertive behavior in business is the key to empowering leaders, increasing employee engagement, and improving accountability.
8. Using assertive behavior in our personal lives helps to create strong, healthy relationships based on trust that can withstand the ups and downs of life.
9. Assertiveness is all about respect: having it ourselves and expecting it from others.
10. If the people in our lives are unwilling to accept our assertiveness, then we have serious choices to make about the future of those relationships.

chapter
four

THE
AGGRESSIVE STYLE

When you hear the word "aggressive," what comes to mind?

Football players. Soldiers. Irritable drivers. People with perfume samples in department stores.

All of those could technically apply. But I want to refine the meaning of that word as it relates to the aggressive style of communication. Aggressives in this context aren't just strong or powerful; they are overbearing and intimidating. Angry and belittling. Hurtful and deceptive. They fail to acknowledge our rights, needs, or concerns in their constant attempts to make us give in, give up, or give out. They are persistently manipulative— and they will stop at nothing to get their way.

> # Aggressives are addicted to drama. Big time!

No wonder Aggressives can drive us crazy. Communication with them is almost impossible. Relationships with them are perpetually stressful. They love to play games with everyone around them by using their favorite tools: **hurt and anger.**

"Stop right there. Are you saying I'm aggressive if I express hurt and anger?"

Not at all. You can be assertive and display those same feelings. Assertives do NOT need to stay in perfect control of their emotions at all times. That's a huge misconception.

People experience genuine hurt and deep sorrow all the time. It's a natural, human response to many situations. The death of a loved one. The loss of a job. The betrayal of a friend or partner. Life can be difficult sometimes. Those events automatically trigger a sense of hurt, and it's perfectly normal to express sadness and grief.

Releasing pent-up anger can be necessary for our well-being, too—even downright therapeutic. Just as there are meaningful and appropriate times to be hurt, there are also situations where anger is justified. Losing the data for your presentation when the whole network crashes. Being cut off in traffic. Discovering your biggest client switched to your competitor. Stuff happens, right?

Assertive hurt and anger, however, are different from manipulative hurt and anger.

Assertive hurt and anger are emotional expressions without any intent to manipulate another person into doing what you want.

Instead, these emotions are a way to move into problem-solving mode. They are backed up by fairness, integrity, and consistency.

"I'm hurt that my company decided to let me go during the downsizing. But I'm going to update my resumé and get an even better job next time."

"I'm angry about what happened, and I don't want it to happen again. But let's figure out how to fix this problem and move on."

"Good to know. So how do Aggressives use anger and hurt?"

ANGER

People who use aggressive anger to get their needs met resort to the more volatile forms of manipulation. These Aggressives are hard-core bullies. They threaten, yell, scream, slam doors, give dirty looks, use blatant sarcasm, and make condescending statements. Nothing is off limits when they are on a roll. It's loud. Explosive. Scary.

"You are totally incompetent. If you don't complete this assignment, you're fired!"

"Apparently, you don't really care about this contract. You better deliver the products today. Or else."

"I don't know why I even stay. You're pathetic. And I guarantee you'll never find anyone else to put up with you."

Their primary objective is to intimidate us. To make us feel powerless, out of control, and afraid of what they might do. The idea of NOT giving in to their demands may seem even more frightening. That could lead to a nasty fight or a major struggle or a heated debate. Much too uncomfortable. It would be better to go with the flow and help prevent the next catastrophic meltdown.

Aggressives love that thought process.

NOTICE THE CONTRAST:

Aggressive anger is manipulative. It is NOT mature,

confident, wise, or rational. Instead, it's generally unfair, hostile, and threatening, which renders the unassertive opponent incapable of responding. It intimidates others with fear and bullies them into submission.

Assertive anger, on the other hand, doesn't involve blames, threats, or attacks on another person's character. The anger is real and honest, but it is communicated with an attempt to find a mutually beneficial solution and maintain a healthy relationship with the other person.

HURT

People who act hurt to get their needs met are the ones we might describe as whiners, complainers, sad sacks and, of course, victims. But they want much more than our sympathy. They want us to feel responsible for their choices, their mistakes, or their situations.

"I never would have thought about hurt as an aggressive ploy."

It's not as obvious but every bit as powerful. Keep in mind:

Manipulation is defined as trying to change the behavior of someone through abusive, deceptive, or underhanded tactics.

Purposefully acting hurt to make someone else feel responsible is manipulation in the first degree. Guilty as charged.

Think about it. If we feel responsible for a problem, that usually results in guilt. And guilt propels us to action. Even accountability. Suddenly we're willing to meet their needs and do whatever they want—even if the issue isn't our fault or the solution isn't in our best interests.

"I can't afford to miss another deadline. But it's not fair that everyone else gets to go home early while I'm still here slaving away."

"You know I have a lot going on in my personal life right now. How can you still expect me to turn in reports on time?"

"No one ever helps me around here."

"Obviously you don't love me or you would know how I am feeling."

Aggressives who use hurt are counting on us to be overwhelmed with empathy (or worn down by the whining). They are hoping we give in to avoid any more guilt being thrown our way.

"You poor thing! Of course I can pitch in to make sure this job gets done."

Score one for the Aggressives. Even though we know they wasted most of the day texting friends instead of working, we've now taken responsibility for the problem. We're willing to take action to resolve it. We actually feel compelled to rescue these helpless victims. But rest assured, there's nothing helpless about them. They are strategically trying to manipulate our emotions until we give in and do whatever they want.

LET'S RECAP:

> **People who use HURT to manipulate want us to feel GUILTY.**
> **People who use ANGER to manipulate want us to feel FEAR.**

In both cases, their goal is to make those emotions so intense for us that we'll take ownership of their problems. We end up doing whatever it takes to get rid of the shameful, overwhelming feelings produced by the guilt or intimidation they laid on us.

"I understand the power of fear. But why is guilt so effective as a manipulator?"

Think about times when you've felt guilty. Terrible feeling, right? You said something wrong. You were at fault in a given situation (even if it was unintentional). The experience replays over and over in your mind, becoming more traumatic with every mental screening. Why did you do that? What should you have done differently? What are the other people thinking about you now?

> # Guilt works at the subconscious level, which makes it the perfect saboteur.

It doesn't take long before you start doubting your choices and decisions. You feel inadequate and unworthy, which seems to welcome in other crippling emotions. Add in a heaping cup of anxiety and a pint of worrying about the future, and you've got the perfect pot of guilt stew.

No wonder we avoid guilt at all costs. That's exactly what the Aggressives are counting on!

"Do men and women use the aggressive style differently?"

My experience does show that women resort to using hurt and guilt more often to get their needs met than men do. As young girls, they typically receive the message that it's acceptable to express emotions like sadness, and they generally get way more positive attention when they are crying than boys do.

Boys are more likely to be told that crying is unacceptable. They learn to express themselves using loud voices and even physical contact. Females might be reprimanded for that kind of behavior, but males are accepted with comments like "boys will be boys."

> **Interestingly enough, our typical socialization training creates a perfect (but unhealthy) match in the world of imperfect relationships.**

Women tend to give in more when confronted by anger, and men often cave in when confronted by tears and sadness. That whole *Venus/Mars* thing is often the reality that's in play.

Of course, there are always exceptions to those broad generalities. In therapy sessions, I have worked with plenty of angry, even abusive women and sad, guilt-producing men. But men and women—on average—do tend to have some deep-seated communication patterns that fall along some stereotypical lines.

With that said, we're beginning to see some changes in those patterns over time. Professional women understand that tears and hurt feelings won't help them get ahead at work (or at home, for that matter). Men are learning that anger doesn't garner the respect they need to advance their careers, and it can quickly erode their personal relationships. There's definitely a behavior shift under way.

The good news is that we can all learn to recognize our natural communication patterns and use that understanding to avoid becoming the Aggressives' target.

"OK, so how can I tell if an Aggressive is trying to manipulate me?"

Excellent question.

> **When you are confronted by someone who is angry or hurt, the way to determine the intent of those emotions is to check your own gut reaction.**

Do you feel genuine empathy for this person who is going through a hard time? Or are the strong emotions making you feel guilty, insecure, afraid, and inadequate? Does it seem like this person wants YOU to take responsibility for the problems? Are you feeling the pressure to "save them"?

Feeling empathy is one thing; feeling cornered is another. And it's a big red flag. In that case, there might as well be a flashing neon sign: "Manipulation in Progress."

"Any other clues?"

Listen to the language, specifically the way people begin their sentences. Assertives rely on "I," while Aggressives attack with "You."

"I sentences" take responsibility for feelings and choices. They aren't attacking or placing blame.

"You sentences" criticize, complain, intimidate, and threaten.

HERE ARE SOME EXAMPLES:

AGGRESSIVE

"You are delusional if you think I'm going to keep covering for you because you have personal problems. You do nothing around here, and then you expect the rest of us to pick up the pieces! You are really inconsiderate."

ASSERTIVE

"I understand that you're having some problems at home right now, but I'm frustrated that so much of your time is spent on personal phone calls. I'm having to pick up your extra work as a result, and I'd like to discuss some ways to split things up more evenly."

AGGRESSIVE

"You haven't finished the report?! You're responsible for one of our best customers, and you're forcing them to delay signing the contract. You better not be counting on a raise this year!"

ASSERTIVE

"I know there was a short turnaround time for this last project, but I was counting on the materials you committed to deliver. The client is waiting, and I need the report ASAP."

AGGRESSIVE

"You obviously don't love me anymore. You never talk to me or consider my feelings. You never want to spend time with me, and you seem to prefer being at the office. You have no idea how much you've hurt me."

ASSERTIVE

"I feel bad that we haven't been getting along lately. I remember how we used to talk and help each other. I know I haven't been as sensitive as I should be, and I'd like to change the way things are."

"So I just need to listen to the first words of their sentences? Great!"

Not so fast. While the "I vs. You" language is a great guideline, it's not completely foolproof. Difficult people can be tricky.

I remember a woman who attended one of my seminars on assertiveness in which we discussed the value of using "I sentences." When she returned a week later for the follow-up session, she was proud to announce that she had implemented this new technique.

We all congratulated her and asked her to describe what happened. She then relayed her conversation with an employee who had come in late.

"I'm so annoyed with you right now. I think you are completely irresponsible. I'm tired of your inability to follow the rules, and I suggest you decide whether you want to keep this job!"

Perhaps a premature celebration on that one. She was technically using the "I sentences," but those messages were definitely "You." Word choice is important, but intent takes the main stage.

"OK, why would anyone actually choose the aggressive style? It seems so...mean."

If we're honest, we can probably think of a time or two in our own lives when we used some type of aggressive communications. We all have; it just happens. We're human. *(No, you don't have to admit that out loud.)* The problem arises when it's a consistent pattern.

Aggressives didn't wake up one morning and just decide to adopt a hostile personality. It probably started when they were children, adding to those mental filing cabinets we discussed in Chapter One. Instead of a conscious choice, it was a long process of trial and error.

They discovered that aggressive communications produced the best results for getting their needs met, so they repeated them. Again and again. And other people *(sorry...maybe even YOU)* helped them to refine those skills and master this unpleasant art.

Aggressives begin to see others as their adversaries: people standing in the way of getting what they want. Whoever is in the way must be dealt with and rendered defenseless. That's the battle they are constantly waging. Control for them is the same as survival.

"Here's the bigger question. Why do people repeatedly allow Aggressives to manipulate them?"

There are three main reasons.

1. THEY LACK THE SKILLS TO STOP THE MANIPULATION.

It's simply not a skill set they possess.

More specifically, they don't know how to neutralize the Aggressives by using assertive behavior and responding to them with constructive feedback. Maybe they are even addicted to the drama. They wouldn't know what to do without it, so they never had an incentive to learn new skills that would change the pattern.

Once they understand how to implement those approaches, they can begin to change the dynamics of the relationship. *(Teaser: the next chapter includes the full game plan for that.)*

2. THEY LACK THE MINDSET TO BREAK THE PATTERN.

It's heartbreaking. Some people think so little of themselves that they are willing to believe what others say *(even mean people!)* rather than focus on what they know to be true about themselves.

That really explains why inappropriate, unhealthy communication exists. The abusers can't do it by themselves. They need the help of those who are willing to allow it, accept it, and even reward it. On some level, the people on the receiving end decide it's normal. It's acceptable. Even merited.

> **People generally treat us the way we allow ourselves to be treated.**

Yes, I know. You've read this before. But it's so important that it deserves repeating.

If you're thinking there must be exceptions to the treatment rule, you're right. Certain categories of people—like children and victims of crimes—have no choice about how they are treated. They are tragically thrown into terrible situations over which they have no control. Whole different conversation.

The discussion here concerns people who actually have a CHOICE about allowing the manipulation to continue. They stay at a job with a terrible boss because they don't want to do what it takes to find a better place of employment. They keep working with an abusive client because they claim they can't meet quota without that sale. They continue in a horrible relationship because they are afraid of being alone. *(The reality is, if you're in a bad relationship, you're alone most of the time anyway.)*

> **There is nothing lonelier than being in a relationship with someone who doesn't like, respect, or believe in you.**

On the surface, the rationalizations that hold us back might seem valid. But people stuck in difficult relationships with Aggressives can't even visualize the alternatives. They don't see any choices at all, just a frightening dead end with nowhere to turn. They actually think they *deserve* to be stuck, and they don't feel *worthy* of choices.

But guess what? The alternatives are out there. They could actually find another job or client or significant other. They deserve better. They deserve more courtesy and respect. That realization alone can be the first step in changing the way they manage their relationships, particularly with the Aggressives in their lives.

3. THEY LACK CONFIDENCE TO STAND UP FOR THEMSELVES.

Even if people get to the point of identifying options and believing they deserve better, they simply may not have the courage and confidence to stand up for themselves and choose another alternative. They're essentially paralyzed by their overwhelming feelings of fear and guilt. They even recognize their own inability to take action, which further tanks their declining self-respect. But to them, pushing back seems rude. Unnecessarily confrontational.

"I get that. But isn't it better sometimes to not make waves and just be nice?"

We were all taught to "be nice" in Kindergarten, but somehow that friendly little rule became warped and stretched beyond recognition. Here's my opinion on that subject.

Stop thinking "nice" means you have to be a doormat. Or totally helpless. Or that you can't tell people how you feel.

That's a very unhealthy, limiting definition of "nice." Wherever you found that, just toss the whole dictionary. Being nice is NOT about allowing yourself to be mistreated or disrespected.

Right here, right now, we're going to expand the definition of NICE:

- It's nice to be honest.
- It's nice to let someone know where they stand with you.
- It's nice to set fair limits and expectations so other people can learn to grow and take responsibility for themselves.
- It's nice to graciously advocate to get your own needs met.
- It's nice to be confident.

That's right, you heard it here: **it's NICE to be confident.** People who have a history of being the doormat for Aggressives need to make a change. Step up. Stand up. Speak up. If you don't, you're a target.

Aggressives have a real talent for identifying people with **low levels of assertiveness skills, self-esteem, and confidence.** And when they spot someone who qualifies for the "Most Manipulatable" list, they swoop in to take advantage of a golden opportunity. Don't be that person.

{
REALITY CHECK

Aggressives are all manipulation, no apologies. They provide anger and hurt; you get fear and an endless guilt trip.

#worstvacationever
}

SUMMARY
Points to Remember

1. People who communicate with the aggressive style use hurt and anger to manipulate others.
2. Aggressives use anger to make us feel intimidated and afraid so we will give in to avoid further confrontation.
3. Aggressives use hurt to make us feel guilty so that we take responsibility for their problems.
4. Hurt and anger can be normal, legitimate emotions when manipulation is not the end goal.
5. Aggressives choose to use their manipulative behavior because that was historically the best way to get their needs met.
6. Men and women tend to use (and respond to) aggressive behavior in different ways, although the typical gender differences are shifting.
7. We can determine whether someone is being aggressive with hurt or anger by using a "gut check" (do we feel empathy or manipulation?) and through a language check (are they primarily using *"I sentences"* or *"You sentences"*?).
8. *"I sentences"* are assertive and take responsibility for feelings and choices without attacking or placing blame.
9. *"You sentences"* are aggressive and involve criticizing, complaining, intimidating, and threatening.

10. People reluctantly accept the difficult behavior of Aggressives because they lack the skills to stop the manipulation, the mindset to break the pattern, and the confidence to stand up for themselves.

chapter
five

DEALING WITH AGGRESSIVES

Now that you understand how and why Aggressives do what they do, it's time to learn some strategies to stop the manipulation, fear, guilt, and intimidation.

Before we get started, I want to explain why these strategies really MATTER.

Avoiding or ignoring these anger-wielding, hurt-flaunting Aggressives can make you sick. Mentally. Physically. Emotionally. And psychologically.

> ## Aggressives can seriously poison you with guilt or paralyze you with fear. They are toxic to the body. The heart. The mind. And the soul.

Your health may actually be at risk if you don't make some changes to minimize your chronic stress and anxiety. Long-term stress often produced by guilt and fear has been scientifically proven as a contributing factor to:

- Headaches
- Stomach pain
- Depression
- Fatigue
- Inflammation
- Gastrointestinal disorders
- Cardiovascular disease
- Immune system problems

Experiencing any of those symptoms? Often chronic stress can be traced back to people or situations that cause you to constantly question yourself in a critical, negative way.

"That's serious stuff. Could be dangerous."

Scary, right? This chapter has the solutions you need. Stay with me here...

> ## To change the pattern of your communications with Aggressives, you have to take control and change YOUR response.

Remember, we can't change other people. But we can change our words, actions, and reactions in a way that no longer allows their needs to get met through manipulation. That process can transform the relationship.

Ready to make a change? Let's look at **three strategies** you can use when dealing with Aggressives.

1. LEARN NEW SKILLS

Sometimes it helps to dig deeper and analyze your typical communications with Aggressives on a more granular level. Think about past interactions with aggressive people and look for patterns. Break it down.

- What did they say or do?
- How did you respond?
- What were the results?
- Did they get their needs met?
- How did you feel?
- Did that sequence recur?

These questions aren't usually top-of-mind in the middle of

an angry confrontation, but the answers may help you realize why you're a frequent passenger on the manipulation train.

No big secret here. If you want to take back control of your relationships with Aggressives, you need to learn the **assertive communication style.** Chapter Three: read, rinse, repeat.

Study the characteristics of the assertive approach, and begin incorporating them into your life (at work and at home). Practice. Stick with it. Identify an assertive role model who can give you inspiration.

Next, think about the way you give **feedback** to Aggressives in your life. Assertives are experts at using constructive feedback to their advantage to change the interactive pattern.

Choices for responding to Aggressives:

POSITIVE FEEDBACK:
No. You don't want to reinforce bad behavior.

CONSTRUCTIVE FEEDBACK:
YES! You want to acknowledge behavior that needs to stop and encourage positive change.

DESTRUCTIVE FEEDBACK:
No. You don't want to participate in equally bad behavior.

AVOIDANCE:
No. You don't want to condone their negative behavior and set them up to do it again.

No contest. The hands-down winner is the constructive style. To begin changing the tone of your interactions with Aggressives, study that approach. Practice it. Use it consistently.

One final note. Once the Aggressives begin to make progress, you can always use positive feedback to reward and encourage their adjustments. *(Well, right after you give yourself a big ol' high five for moving toward the awesomely assertive relationship you want!)*

2. SHIFT YOUR THINKING

To become more assertive when communicating with Aggressives, you have to start changing the way you think. In other words, you need to reprogram your mind and convince yourself that you're worthy of open, honest, respectful communications and healthy relationships.

I realize this might seem like a daunting task. And why not? It makes perfect sense that your self-esteem might be sagging a bit: you've been repeatedly bullied by an Aggressive! I'm guessing you've spent way more than your fair share of time on the receiving end of hurt, guilt, anger, sarcasm, contempt, martyrdom, silent treatments, rants, blame, ridicule, and criticism. That would take an enormous toll on ANYBODY.

On some level, you probably even realize you're being mistreated, which only reinforces the guilt and the shame. If you repeatedly get the message that you're inadequate, you start to believe it. And repeat it.

Erasing those "old tapes" will take some time and effort, but it's possible. You can do this!

Self-evaluation is the starting point. You want to gain a thorough understanding of how and why you feel, think, and communicate the way you do.

Conscious decisions almost always take more thought and planning. But if you want to gain control over your difficult relationships, you have to mentally make a change: commit to the concept of implementing different choices that can transform your relationship. All in. No doubt.

Without this full shift, the difficult people in your life will see right through your half-hearted attempts to use assertive communication techniques. They'll sense that you aren't being authentic.

I'm not kidding here. There's a 99.9% chance that difficult people are going to call your bluff when you try to make changes. And that's probably a conservative estimate.

You can yell *"I don't deserve this!"* over and over, but difficult people are masters at reading the deeper message. Experience tells them that you aren't serious. You're tentative. They can tell you don't really believe it, and there's no way you're going to back that up. If they sense any internal hesitancy on your part below the assertive facade, they'll do everything in their power to get you to backtrack.

> ## If you want others to respect you, you have to start by respecting yourself.

- Recognize that you deserve to have positive, healthy relationships.
- Understand that you have choices about the way you are treated in your relationships.

- Remember that you NEVER have to be bullied, threatened, intimidated, or manipulated.
- Realize that positive choices will protect you from long-term, health-zapping emotions like guilt and shame.
- Believe that you are worthy of respect.

Once you adopt that attitude, you'll begin to radiate confidence through your voice, gestures, tone, and body language. And when that happens, the difficult people in your life will do much more than just hear your words and see your actions. They'll begin to feel the change in you that says, *"I am a valuable person, and I will be treated respectfully."* That's what gets their attention.

Assertives project their confidence from the inside out.

"I'm guessing that mental shift won't go over well with the Aggressives."

Oddly enough, boosting your self-respect may actually give you greater credibility with the Aggressives. Even though they are actively trying to get their needs met by manipulating you, they also lose respect for you when you let them get away with it. How's that for hypocrisy? It's fair to say that they won't be big fans of the change at first, but that's what just might fuel the relationship transformation.

Once some Aggressives begin to realize that you expect fair and ethical treatment, their need and desire to play games with you will be lessened considerably. Some difficult people can actually be quite cooperative, polite, and accommodating in relationships with people they respect. What a concept, right? But continuing to be bullied by them or ignoring their unacceptable behavior will simply increase the odds that they treat you badly long-term.

When I was working at a large hospital, one particular doctor was clearly an Aggressive. He was known for bullying the nurses. When he walked into the room, everyone would scurry away to avoid his wrath. Except for one nurse. She assertively refused to allow herself to be treated badly. She didn't fight or yell or engage in power struggles. But she didn't back down.

Amazingly, the doctor was respectful in his conversations with her. He even said *"please"* and *"thank you."* He could read her emotional boundaries from a mile away.

For all of the other nurses, it looked like an absolute miracle. But that's what happens when you combat aggressive behavior with a firm, assertive style. It all starts with believing that you are worthy of more.

Assertives are mentally tough. They know they don't deserve to be treated badly, and they won't accept it. They deal with it up front. Is it time for you to draw a line in the sand?

---

3. CHANGE THE WAY YOU ACT AND REACT

You've studied the process. You've convinced yourself that you deserve better. Now it's time to exude your new sense of confidence—from the inside out. Speak up. Stand up. Set boundaries and limits. Make a different choice. Be assertive, and don't back down when Aggressives dig in their heels.

"Should I tell the Aggressive person that things are about to change?"

Assertives know how to clearly explain to others what is expected, sometimes even encouraging them to participate in the process of setting those expectations. While people do deserve information about changes that will impact them, you'll want to handle Aggressives with extra care.

Here are two examples of ways to approach this transition: the **wrong way** (aggressive) and the **right way** (assertive).

AGGRESSIVE (NO!)

"Things are going to be different. Starting today! I'm adopting an assertive communication style, and I refuse to put up with your antics anymore. I deserve better!"

ASSERTIVE (YES!)

"In the past, I have overlooked some of the rules where you're concerned, but I've realized that's not productive for either one of us. I'm now setting some firm parameters and deadlines that apply

to everyone in the department. If you have any questions about that, I would be happy to answer them."

Honestly, don't be too surprised if your initial assertive statement prompts some smiles (or even full-blown laughter) from your Aggressives. They know your track record. They simply aren't going to believe your out-of-character statements until you demonstrate that your confidence has staying power.

Confront the issue. Calmly stick to your guns. The Aggressives will eventually figure out that you aren't practicing lines from a play.

"I think I'm a little fuzzy on the difference between confronting and being confrontational."

Very good point.

When you **confront** an issue or a problem, you deal with it confidently. You face it. Address it. Accept the challenge.

If you're **confrontational**, you purposely create a hostile or argumentative interaction with the intent to escalate the conflict.

> ## Assertives confront; Aggressives are confrontational.

Some people would rather do almost anything than be involved in a confrontation. Get a root canal. Give up tickets to the Super Bowl. Go grocery shopping the day before Thanksgiving. Really, anything. Confrontations cause them an enormous amount of stress, so their first instinct is to minimize the pain by ignoring or giving in to their demands. *"Why make the situation any worse?"*

Assertives have learned that confronting is the only way to neutralize the problem. Even the positive, proactive form of confronting may be out of your comfort zone (OK, possibly even several zones away), but you'll come to realize that the honesty and openness of confronting assertively are instant stress relievers. It's actually quite liberating.

As you begin using more assertive techniques, Aggressives will likely try their best to change your confronting into a confrontational event. But don't panic when you start to feel guilt or fear gripping your heart. It will be very tempting to go for the instant, react-and-move-on response that works well as a confrontation-stopper. And why not? That's always been a great way to make the guilt vanish: turn a "no" into a "yes" by doing what they ask, meeting their demands, and giving up the battle.

Stop! Listen when you hear your inner assertive communicator screaming, *"Hang in there! We can deal with this!"* Don't give in. Don't let your confronting become confrontational. Focus on the potential for long-term results before abandoning your rational mind.

"Once I set the ground rules with the Aggressives, then what? Is there a strategy I can use?"

Explaining the new system to functional, balanced, assertive human beings would be one thing; trying to implement change with difficult, irrational people who think they play by different rules is an entirely different challenge.

HERE'S THE GENERAL GAME PLAN:

- Ask the person to discuss the issue with you.
- State your needs without accusing or attacking.
- Remain focused on the topic.
- Avoid defensiveness, excuses, or apologies (unless warranted).
- Stand firm.

"That sounds almost too easy. So what's the catch?"

You knew that was coming, didn't you? Aggressives are masters of the detour, and you need to protect yourself from being forced to make unintended turns in your conversations. They will purposely try to get you off the subject so they can control the discussion and follow their own agendas. Every time we choose to follow their detours and go off-topic, we become more lost. Stick to your original GPS game plan!

Here's a classic detour example in a business setting:

Blair: *"David, I need to talk to you about your tardiness. Work starts at 8:00, and today you came in at 8:20. I need you to be on time."*

David: *"Well, everyone is late once in a while, and you never call them out. What about Nancy? She's never on time."* **(detour)**

Blair: *"Nancy has had some personal problems, and we've already discussed her scheduling issues."* **(took the detour; now defending)**

David: *"Besides, you're always picking on me. Nothing I do is ever right."* **(detour)**

Blair: *"That's not true. I'm very pleased with the work you're doing."* **(took the detour; now supporting)**

David: *"And you never notice all the times I'm here working long after everyone else has left. I think a lot of people take advantage of me."* **(detour)**

Blair: *"Well, I'm sorry you feel that way, David. Just try to be on time from now on."* **(took the detour; apologizes; reframes the command as a suggestion)**

Seriously?! TRY to be on time? What started out as an assertive conversation to definitively correct David's tardiness ends with Blair suggesting punctuality would be a lovely idea. Major detours there. Like the GPS had a complete and total meltdown. Aggressives know how to do that so masterfully. They turn the tables and, before we know it, we are the ones backing off, defending, and apologizing.

"I've definitely seen that before. What's the solution?"

To avoid detours, be more observant. Think about what you need to say, how you want to say it, and stick to the subject. Your subject, not theirs. Remember that assertiveness requires you to be proactive about your conversations rather than reactive.

> # When someone tries to take you on a detour, use the age-old "broken record" technique to stay on track.

"Interesting...what exactly is the broken record?"

The name comes from a common issue that used to happen when playing old-fashioned vinyl records. If a record was scratched, the needle would get stuck and repeat one section of the song over and over again. We've eliminated that problem today with our digital downloads from the iTunes Store, but the concept still comes in quite handy in dealing with Aggressives and their need to navigate every conversation.

Returning to the previous example, Blair could have used this approach to maintain control of her conversation with David:

Blair: *"David, I need you to be at work on time promptly at 8:00."*
David: *"But..."* **(detour)**
Blair: *"No, I need you to be here on time."* **(broken record)**
David: *"Nancy is always late..."* **(detour)**
Blair: *"Right now, we are talking about you. I need you here on time."* **(broken record)**

You don't need to make excuses, defend yourself, or apologize. Just state your needs firmly and repeat them, if necessary. If you don't get their attention, then you may need to add a consequence and let them know assertively what will happen if the behavior doesn't change.

> Blair: *"David, I don't get the feeling you are hearing me about the importance of being on time. If you anticipate being late again, we can discuss a solution to help prevent that from happening. But if it does happen again, I will issue a written warning."*

The same approach of detour-avoidance works at home, too.

> Mom: *"Your curfew tonight is midnight."*
> Jenna: *"But Mom, the party doesn't even start until 10!"* **(detour)**
> Mom: *"Midnight has always been your curfew, and that isn't changing this year."* **(broken record)**
> Jenna: *"Shelby's parents are letting her stay out later..."* **(detour)**
> Mom: *"That's nice, but you're not Shelby. The curfew is midnight."* **(broken record)**
> Jenna: *"You know I'm very responsible. Remember when I came home early the night of the storm and..."* **(detour)**
> Mom: *"Jenna, your curfew is midnight. If you choose not to accept the responsibility to be on time, then you will not be able to go out with your friends at all next weekend."* **(broken record)**

Assertive communications get the job done. While it's not always easy to spell out the consequences, it's a necessary part of healthy relationships. If you want what is best for yourself and the people you care about, assertiveness is the only way to make that happen.

"What should I do if the Aggressive person's behavior gets worse?"

YOU HAVE TO STAND YOUR GROUND. ASSERTIVELY.

I remember watching an interesting television documentary about bears. The animal experts described the best thing to do if you come face-to-face with a bear. Their suggestion is probably easier said than done, but they recommended standing still and looking the bear right in the eyes to let it know you're not afraid. According to the experts, that act of confidence increases the chance that the bear will walk away and not attack you. But if the animal senses that you are afraid, inferior, or confused, you're much more likely to...well, become the bear's tasty lunch entree.

The same advice holds true for dealing with Aggressives. And I don't know about you, but I think it would be MUCH easier to stand up to a difficult person rather than an angry bear. *(If you feel like the threat level is about the same right now, I'm really glad you're reading this book!)*

As soon as Aggressives know that you are fearful, upset, or inadequate, they will increase their attacks. But if they DON'T get that reaction, you leave them no choice but to reconsider how they communicate with you.

Stand up. Face the bear, and deliver your message again. This is the true test. And whatever you do, don't apologize for standing up.

"What do you mean by that?"

When Aggressives are pushing hard with anger and detours, even the most confident people may begin to slip into apologetic mode.

"I'm sorry, but the report is due."

"I'm sorry, but I need you to attend the meeting."

"I'm sorry, but I believe midnight is a fair curfew."

"I'm sorry, but I need you to arrive on time for class."

It's a common habit. But why should anyone apologize when asking for something that is right and fair? For Aggressives, those statements seem like a big, beautiful, open door. *"Awesome! They already feel sorry. I can walk right in and take charge!"*

Let's make a very important point about apologies. The words, *"I am sorry,"* can be three of the strongest words in the English language—or three of the weakest.

An apology should only be given when one of the following two things is true:

- You made a serious mistake.
- You never intend to repeat the behavior.

Look back and reread those previous apology statements. It's not a mistake to ask people to adhere to the rules. And if they don't comply, it's perfectly acceptable to bring up the issue again. There are natural consequences for failing to cooperate or perform. If you're in a position of authority, you have a right to expect certain behavior and ask for it (and continue asking for it until you get it). No apologies needed.

> **Using the words "I'm sorry" weakens your boundary setting and plays right into the difficult person's hands.**

Difficult people have a lifetime of success playing their manipulation games. If you apologize, they will sense some weakness. Definitely not the message you want to send. Thankfully, you now know how to calmly and firmly use the broken-record technique. It's a strategy that WILL work if used consistently.

That's my way of saying that difficult people may be momentarily stunned when they encounter someone who is willing or able to stand up to them, but they probably won't be ready to relinquish control immediately.

"More confrontation? Really?!"

Perhaps initially, but don't give up.

If you feel the urge to cave in, stop and congratulate yourself for being assertive. The fact that the Aggressives are ramping up means that your efforts are working. Give yourself a well-deserved pat on the back with a bonus pep talk:

1. You have made a smart choice to be assertive with your relationships.
2. You are remaining in control despite pushback.
3. You are not allowing yourself to be mistreated or manipulated.
4. You haven't given in to their demands.
5. You have not resorted to their aggressive tactics.
6. Your self-esteem level is higher.
7. You have more confidence in your tone and demeanor.
8. Your perseverance will lead to healthy, positive relationships.

Aggressives might be fighting back against your assertiveness, but they will begin to do it with less swagger and a begrudging admiration for your new self-respect. Assertiveness is comforting to be around, even for the difficult person. You'll begin to feel better. And they will, too.

"So how long will it take for Aggressives to adjust their behavior?"

That depends. Every situation is different. The good news is, assertiveness usually does improve the situation in the long run when used consistently. And when it does, the results are wonderful. You get a chance to live or work in a vastly improved environment with someone who previously caused great stress and tension.

- If you're an executive who needs to fire an employee, you can plan out a series of assertive conversations to help that person exit with the least amount of emotional upheaval (or lawsuits).
- If you're a team leader, you can start modeling and supporting assertive communications to create a more productive group that operates based on trust and respect.
- If you're a parent, you can begin using assertive communications with children to establish boundaries that will keep them safe and give them a crucial framework for becoming successful adults.
- If you have a significant other, you can create a healthier, happier relationship where both of you feel valued and confident in your contribution to the partnership.

It's worth the wait. But the honest truth? Some people may never get better, which leaves you with an important decision to make. If you've exhausted every assertive technique and the Aggressives won't budge, you have three options:

1. ***Stay in the relationship,*** accept the situation "as is," and stop complaining. In other words, you are willing

to agree to their rules for communication, and you understand that you are a partner in the dysfunction.

2. ***Make a plan to get help or look for other options.*** You may not be able to quit the job, leave the relationship, or stop talking to a "friend" immediately, but you know something has to change—and that change must start with YOU.

3. ***Sever the relationship*** because the situation is unacceptable. You are in a position to get out, quit, or leave right away. You take action, and you make the commitment to learn more about yourself so you won't be attracted to another difficult person or situation in the future.

That's not harsh. It's simply the facts. You know you did your best, but it's senseless to continue to waste your time and energy on a potentially destructive situation. You acted maturely and responsibly. You can move on to a healthier place in life without wondering if you did everything you could to salvage the relationship.

Becoming assertive isn't a simple solution, but it's the only one that will enable a relationship that is happy, successful, and free from angry confrontations.

{
REALITY CHECK

Move over, Aggressives. We're standing up and speaking out. The manipulation stops here!

#bullieslose
}

SUMMARY
Action Plan: *Dealing with Aggressives*

1. Commit to making a change! To protect your emotional and physical health, you have to stop being controlled by the aggressive people in your life.

2. Learn to be more assertive, boost your self-esteem, and increase your confidence to begin transforming your relationships with Aggressives.

3. Use assertive communication and constructive feedback to get the best responses from Aggressives.

4. Reprogram your thought processes to convince yourself that you are worthy of respect. Long periods of manipulation may have damaged your self-esteem.

5. Assertively state your needs, begin setting boundaries, and explain your expectations for how you want to be treated. Aggressives will start to take notice.

6. Stand your ground when Aggressives challenge you. Refuse to back down, fall for their intimidation, or take their emotional detours.

7. Avoid getting distracted by using the broken-record technique to stay on track. Remain focused and keep repeating your message.

8. Resist apologizing when you restate your positions.

9. Be firm and consistent about changing the relationship formula.

10. Retrain the Aggressives in your life to treat you better. It will take some time, but the benefits will be outstanding.

What if **YOU** *might be the Aggressive person?*

1. Recognize that you can't reach your full potential for success without using the assertive style. Accept that, and make the effort to change. You might feel like you're getting ahead by being aggressive, but you're slowly undermining your progress.

2. Focus on finding win/win solutions. Remind yourself to think about the needs of the people around you, and factor those in to your problem-solving. Others are not the enemy.

3. Try to remove all manipulation from your interactions with others. Focus on honest, direct, collaborative discussions.

4. Put strategies in place to calm down if your temper flares. Try counting to 10, taking a break, walking around the block, or listening to soothing music. Think before you lash out.

5. Stop complaining. Adopt a positive attitude and make it a point to project a "glass half full" attitude.

6. Contrast the short-term satisfaction of aggressively getting your needs met NOW with the broader benefits of behaving more assertively. The long-term advantages of the assertive style will bring you greater success in every area of your life. Make a list. Visualize the differences to keep you motivated.

7. Be honest with others about your attempts to improve your interactions. Others will appreciate knowing that you recognize the problem. Plus, that vulnerability will gain you some respect.

8. Ask for forgiveness if you fall back on old habits (from others and from yourself). Those aggressive techniques are deeply ingrained, and you will continue to make progress over time.

9. Find a mentor or trusted partner to help you practice having assertive conversations. Give them permission to discreetly confront you if you begin reverting to aggressive techniques. Be open to suggestions about ways to improve your interactions.

chapter
six

THE
PASSIVE STYLE

If the difficult people in your life use the passive communication style, you know what it sounds like when they tell you exactly what they need.

Total silence.

Nothing.

Crickets.

Yep, that can be every bit as frustrating as the in-your-face, mow-you-down Aggressives.

We already know that the avoiding and ignoring feedback style is highly ineffective, but the Passives missed that group email. That's their go-to solution for every situation. Why deal with an issue or a person head-on? All of that conflict can be stressful. Plus, it takes so much time and energy. Definitely not worth the hassle, the anguish, and the pain.

> **Passives love the path of least resistance. As a matter of fact, I'm pretty sure they invented it.**

The problem is, Passives are constantly shortchanging themselves. They downplay and undervalue their own opinions, concerns, interests, and needs. They stifle their true personalities so they can be seen as "easy to get along with." However you look at it, Passives tend to be uncomfortable expressing themselves.

In psychology, that's called **lacking a voice.**

HERE ARE A FEW EXAMPLES:

"Luke is the most productive person on my team, but everyone else complains that he is arrogant and annoying. I'm afraid he'll get mad and quit if I say anything, and I don't have time to train another new person. Maybe he'll mellow out eventually."

"I'm frustrated that the group members always ask me to take notes and send out the recaps after the meetings. Can't we rotate that job? I better not say anything though or they'll think I'm not a team player."

"Skylar loves to gossip about other people at work—employees, customers, even our boss. I don't want to hear it, and I don't add anything to the conversation. But I never tell her to stop either. I don't want her to think I'm being judgmental."

"My friend Hannah always wants me to go with her to concerts. Honestly, I can't stand the crowds and all the screaming. I don't know how to tell her that; it might make her mad. She's counting on me, so I go with her anyway—and I hate every single minute."

"My mother expects us to come over to her house every Sunday night for dinner. We are all busy, and the kids have so many activities. We desperately need some downtime as a family. But I don't want to hurt her feelings, so we keep going. Every week."

"Yeah, those people really need to man up and move on."

Not so fast. Before you start throwing shade at those wimpy Passives, ask yourself a few questions:

- Have you ever said "yes" when you meant "no"?
- Have you ever agreed to do something you didn't really want to do?
- Have you ever decided it was easier to just go with what everyone else wants rather than trying to convince them that your idea is better?
- Have you ever given in because you didn't want to hurt others' feelings or make them angry?

So there you have it. Occasionally, we have ALL taken the passive route. For some, it's a brief scenic tour. For others, it's a never-ending highway.

"Passives really need to read that chapter about being assertive. Twice!"

So true. But here's an interesting twist.

> ## Passives actually value the assertive principles...FOR EVERYONE BUT THEMSELVES.

Pretty wacky. For some reason, they don't believe they deserve what they work so hard to ensure for everyone else. Instead, they make the futile attempt to be all things to all people, which leaves them with the short end of the stick.

PASSIVES:

- Avoid saying no and take on way too much.
- Allow themselves to be dumped on and mistreated.
- Position themselves as willing to be taken advantage of.
- Don't let people know what they want, need, or feel.
- Expect others to read their minds.
- Stifle their feelings to the point of physical/emotional damage.

- Act happy but really aren't.
- Play the role of the martyr.
- Take things personally far too often.

All of these choices are actually dishonest and unfair—to themselves and the people around them. Passives understand the Assertives' style, but they just can't seem to apply it to themselves.

"That's a problem. So what makes the Passives tick?"

On the upside, Passives are often very intuitive people. They have a knack for sensing what others need and providing it before they even ask. Who wouldn't want to have someone like that in their lives?

The problem is the unspoken expectation of returning the favor. Passives silently expect everyone else to be equally as intuitive and giving, which is hardly ever the case. That's when the emotional challenge begins.

"Let's see if they can figure out what I'm feeling."

"If these people care about me (like me, respect me, love me), they will know what I need."

Basically, the Passives' co-workers, family members, and friends are being evaluated and graded on their ability to guess what the Passives need and automatically provide it. But unless those people are serious mind readers, they will fail the test. Every time.

The results? Everyone loses. Passives rarely get their needs met.

> ## In the world's giant needs–meeting game, Passives essentially forfeit their right to speak up and have a voice.

They have decided to give up on getting their own needs met. And consequently, they are destined to feel sad, hurt, and let down by others. And the people around them don't fare any better. Colleagues and friends feel confused and frustrated, not even certain why they've caused a problem.

"Are Passives actually afraid of confrontation?"

Yes. And the fear is real. They are afraid of the struggle. The outcome. The backlash. The confrontation. The guilt. They would rather feel sad and helpless than assertively work to get their needs met.

CONFRONTATION SCARES PASSIVES FOR TWO REASONS:

1. They are afraid of the physical and emotional feelings associated with confrontation. Tense situations do trigger physiological changes in the body. Rapid pulse. Shallow breathing. Tightness in the neck and chest. Even when we are communicating assertively, it can be stressful if the other person is not cooperating or playing by the same rules. Passives will do everything in their power to avoid those uncomfortable feelings.
2. Passives are afraid of what might happen if they stand up, speak up, or face situations head-on. Will others become verbally or physically abusive? Or leave them? Fire them? Stop speaking to them? Refuse to be friends with them? Withdraw their love and attention?

Then what? It's overwhelming to think about that confrontational interaction. The other person's response is a frightening unknown, and Passives strongly prefer to operate with defined variables.

"So have these people always been Passives? Or how did that start?"

It all goes back to those mental filing cabinets. At some point in their lives, Passives were "trained" to think that responding assertively was unacceptable. However, the training program could take on several different forms. I'll explain.

NEGATIVE REINFORCEMENT

Passives may have come from families dominated by an aggressive parent or caregiver, so they consistently received negative reinforcement. As young children, the Passives learned that avoiding punishment or criticism required staying quiet and flying below the radar. They grew up in households with commands like:

"Shut up, and do what I say!"

"If I want your opinion, I'll ask for it!"

"Who do you think you are? I'm in charge here."

"Quiet! Children should be seen and not heard."

It didn't take long for children in this environment to prefer the security of fading into the background. Sadly, some Passives were also "trained" with severe punishments or some form of abuse. The message became crystal clear: speaking up can have serious ramifications.

> **For a few Passives, assertiveness wasn't just unacceptable, it was dangerous.**

On the other hand, learning to use the passive style as a survival skill doesn't necessarily have to happen during childhood. Even a few traumatic instances later in life can sometimes convert an individual into a pattern of passive behavior. Verbal abuse from an angry manager. A volatile partner. A condescending professor. We can subconsciously get the message at any age that life would be easier if we withdraw and seek peace at our own expense.

Guilt producers using negative reinforcement have a devious way of making us feel responsible for their situations or blaming us for their problems.

POSITIVE REINFORCEMENT

Some Passives grew up in the opposite environment. They got extra attention for NOT rocking the boat. They didn't necessarily experience negative reactions to their attempts at being assertive, but instead they received positive reinforcement as a reward for their passivity. They heard comments like:

"You're such a good little girl. You never cause a fuss."

"Those other boys are trouble-makers, but you have nice manners."

"Thank you for being so flexible and going along with the plans. I know I can count on you."

"Thank goodness you aren't like your brother. He's always creating problems."

These children discovered a fast, efficient way of earning positive attention. They learned to get the love they wanted and needed by NOT making waves. Go along, get along, be good, do what everyone else wants to do. As classic people-pleasers, these Passives don't avoid confrontation because of fear. They avoid it because they love the attention and praise that comes with the submissive, whatever-you-want-is-fine approach.

> **Bottom line: most Passives grow up either being afraid to speak out or being rewarded for staying quiet.**

Those early experiences of negative or positive reinforcement affect how Passives perceive themselves and choose to communicate as adults. This pattern usually continues throughout their lives unless they make a conscious decision to change the way they interact with others in relationships at work and at home.

"That makes sense. But can't Passives just shake that off as adults and start speaking up?"

Absolutely. But it means changing deeply rooted mindsets, not just communication patterns. Passives usually only see two alternatives to "playing nice": being mean or being selfish. For Passives, those are simply not acceptable options. The problem goes back to setting boundaries.

> ## Assertive, fair boundaries are the foundation for all healthy relationships.

Boundaries are the rules we establish and the limits we set to determine how we treat others—and how we will allow them to treat us, talk to us, and behave around us. Those boundaries are a reflection of our core beliefs and the principles we hold for fair, ethical, and just behavior.

Yeah, boundaries are a really big deal.

From the Passive viewpoint though, setting boundaries feels like inviting confrontation. Oh no, we already know that's scary stuff for Passives. They believe the easiest, politest, and least scary thing to do is let someone else establish the rules of the game. They are happy to play along, but they certainly don't want to make the first move. That would put them in the position of being responsible for the consequences of their own decisions and choices.

So that's how it happens. When Passives believe they don't deserve to set boundaries, they open the borders to anyone and everyone. It's like a giant "Welcome" sign inviting others to move in and take advantage of their gentle nature.

"Sure, I'll finish the whole project tonight if that will help you."

"No, I don't mind doing the extra research for the proposal."

"We can always reschedule date night. You go ahead with your friends."

"It's OK. I'll bring your report up to school right now since you forgot it."

Failing to set boundaries comes with consequences. Here's why. When Passives give up their personal rights, they inevitably harbor some intense feelings: anger, resentment, sadness, shame, guilt, and grief, to name a few.

> **To avoid the fight on the outside, Passives begin an internal battle that could be more destructive than any external confrontation they could ever imagine.**

They take the hit on the inside. They give up, they give in, and they give out. They do what others want rather than what they want.

"That's bound to affect the way they feel about themselves."

In a big way. Passives generally struggle with serious issues related to confidence and self-respect. They are constantly working to put others first, so coming in last becomes a way of life for them. That's the only slot left. They insist it's no big deal. They don't mind. But while they appear to happily go with the flow, they aren't really happy at all. That ushers in the martyr mode, which we all know can be tedious and annoying.

People with healthy levels of self-confidence are able and willing to make consistent, healthy, ethical choices, and they surround themselves with others who think the same way. When people continually make unwise, hurtful, or self-destructive choices, their self-esteem plummets. But they aren't the only ones who get knocked to the ground.

In the Passives' perpetual state of martyrdom, they create a sense of unrest and worry among their peers. The Passives might initially be perceived as extremely kind, but that impression eventually fades. It becomes a full-time job trying to figure out what Passives are thinking. Are they happy or sad? Do they really want to stay or go? Do they agree or not? Can they be trusted to express their true feelings? It's exhausting. Annoying. Those easy-going Passives can turn out to be high-maintenance liabilities.

The Passives begin to sense the growing frustration in the people around them, and they take the blame. Naturally, their confidence levels drop even further, since they assume it must be all their fault. The anger is seldom directed at the people responsible, but inward at themselves. Talk about self-inflicted wounds!

The Passives' constant internal battle sounds like this: *"Do something! No, I can't!"* or *"Say something! No, it's not worth it!"* That message replays over and over, reminding them of what they should have said or wish they had done. But the words and actions never materialize, which piles on more guilt and regret and self-blame. No wonder their confidence hits rock-bottom.

Passives may even promise themselves to handle the situation more assertively next time, but they rarely follow through. They'll scream, *"I just can't take it anymore!"* But inevitably, they do. They take much more. Which reinforces the downward spiral of negative thoughts.

"Don't they eventually hit the breaking point?"

Sometimes, after consistently being mistreated or abused, that victim mentality can bubble up to the surface. They actually complain, but they don't change. They speak up—and then continue right along with their martyrdom and damaging, boundary-free relationships.

> ## Passives "cry wolf" way too often. After a while, everyone tunes them out.

We may hear Passives making comments like this:

"It's not fair."

"I can't believe they always expect me to take care of their problems."

"I was never allowed to treat my parents that way when I was a child."

"Why can't we just get along?"

"Why are people mad at me? I always do whatever they want."

"I don't understand why people treat me so badly when I work so hard to be nice."

I am always suspicious of people who keep talking about how hard they are trying to be nice. Trying not to argue. Trying not to make waves. Trying to get along. In most cases, it shouldn't be that hard. When people value themselves and others, doing the right thing should come naturally. It's not a forced emotion, but a way of life.

For Passives, it doesn't work that way.

> **Physically, Passives are often exhausted.**
>
> **Emotionally, Passives are anxious, worried, nervous, and on edge.**
>
> **Mentally, Passives are waging an internal battle.**

It's a full-time, high-stress job *trying* to please everyone and avoid confrontation. Too bad it doesn't come with workers' comp, because it definitely takes a toll on those who choose this occupation.

Don't get me wrong. I am not saying that it is BAD to be a nice person. That's admirable and even necessary for our society. The world needs more people who are kind, empathetic, and giving. Just not at the expense of taking care of themselves. (Remember the new definition of "nice" in Chapter Four?) When we don't stand up for ourselves, we don't get our needs met—and we pay a deceptively high price. And so do all of those around us.

For Passives to improve their self-esteem, they have to begin adopting an assertive mindset. If they want to respect and care for others, they have to respect, care for, and believe in themselves FIRST.

"I think I'm predominantly assertive in some areas of my life, but passive in others. Is that normal?"

Yes. Completely normal.

> ## We have all communicated and related to others in each of the four styles at some time in our lives.

People often have different styles that are dominant in specific situations or with different people. One style at work and another at home. Or perhaps they use one style with family and another with friends. Or they adjust depending on whether they are talking with men or women. Even some of the most assertive people can analyze their interactions and discover a passive trend in a particular area.

Many women, for example, have taught themselves to be very assertive in their professional lives. They can persuasively promote an idea, stand up to a difficult client, and professionally debate an issue that needs to be resolved. Yet, they may not be nearly as proficient at getting their needs met in their personal relationships. They might resort to passive techniques and wait for their partners or significant others to read their minds. Avoiding or ignoring leads to hurt feelings on both sides.

On the other hand, some men may be highly assertive at work. They share the decision-making, form teams for consensus, and work to resolve and negotiate problems. Yet, some of these same assertive men resort to old aggressive or passive-aggressive techniques in their personal relationships. They yell if something does not go their way, go on the attack if they think they are being nagged, or withdraw and refuse to speak if they feel out of control.

With that said, let's be honest here. Gender differences are breaking down today, and styles are becoming mixed. I am also seeing situations where the assertive professional woman becomes aggressive in the home, or the assertive professional male uses guilt and martyrdom as a passive, manipulative tool with his family. Manipulation seems to know no gender or time limits when it decides to pull out the underhanded tricks.

"Are there times when it's actually good to use the passive approach?"

Most definitely. We have to pick our battles in life, especially today when rage seems to be everywhere: in the workplace, on the roads, in schools, in relationships, in the world. Even though being assertive is the healthiest communication style, sometimes there are matters that simply need to be overlooked so that we can move on to more important issues.

Sure, we always want to strive to be assertive. But that doesn't mean we must constantly confront every little thing we don't like about situations or other people. If minor issues don't compromise our goals, performance, or self-respect, it might even be a sign of emotional maturity to focus on other things.

> **When we maturely and wisely choose to ignore a situation because it doesn't warrant our time and energy, that can be a positive choice.**

Your employee has exceptional performance and is well-liked by everyone on the team, but he does tell really stupid jokes. Does that matter? Probably not.

Your S.O. took the time to cook you a gourmet meal, but she used every single pot and pan in the kitchen. And you're on clean-up duty. Should you complain? Again, probably not.

Passive behavior can also be a particular advantage when we are in the presence of a person who is physically or emotionally out of control. If someone is being irrational, it makes sense to back off and avoid a conflict. However, if we have an ongoing relationship with this person, the assertive approach is the only option for a long-term solution.

"Am I being passive when I compromise?"

Not necessarily. Compromise does require that we give in or let go of something we want, but a true assertive compromise means that we also gain something at the same time. Often, when both parties elect to forgo a battle for the good of the relationship, a stronger alliance emerges.

The trouble for the predominantly passive personality is this. They rarely choose any battle. What they believe to be a compromise is usually giving in with nothing gained or resolved in return. Unless you count the sense of loss, shame, frustration, or anger.

THAT'S THE DIFFERENCE.

> ## Assertives actively choose to compromise or give in on an issue ONLY after weighing all the options and determining that the concession won't compromise their values, rights, and beliefs.

Passives give in as the default response. Why negotiate? That sounds very...confrontational. So they compromise at their own expense, while also compromising their values and ethics. Uh-huh. Remember the part about the crushed self-esteem?

"If someone is shy, does that mean they are passive?"

No. Sometimes quiet people are just taking time to carefully weigh their thoughts and choose their words for the appropriate response. Assertives are great listeners, which often requires them to be quiet so they can hear what others are saying.

> ## Passives are afraid to speak up. Assertives aren't—but that doesn't mean they are extroverts.

I often have people in my audiences who are outwardly quiet, but yet they aren't afraid to ask questions when necessary or offer an opinion when appropriate. Many Assertives wouldn't be classified as talkative, although they are totally capable of standing up to people if they feel something is wrong.

On the other hand, there are plenty of loud, chatty people who are predominantly passive. They talk a lot, but they tend to agree with whatever the majority is saying rather than form their own opinions. These Passives can be very frustrating, especially if you are counting on their support. You think they are in agreement with your ideas and are ready to back you up. They provide their verbal vote of confidence because that's what they think you want to hear. Later, you may discover they have been equally supportive of an opposing view. Textbook passive behavior.

All of that to say, we can't assume all introverts are Passives.

"Sounds like Passives are much more susceptible to peer pressure."

Without a doubt. The more passive people are, the more worried they are about how they are being perceived by those around them. Since they don't want to hurt peoples' feelings or make them angry, they may go along with the crowd to avoid those issues.

The obvious example can be found with children. Those who are taught to be assertive can "just say no" when faced with dangerous or destructive options. But passive children are more susceptible to following the bad behaviors of their peers—lying, skipping school, drinking, taking drugs, shoplifting, you name it. Even bad attitudes. They succumb to the pressure: *"We all do it. You won't get caught. You're a wimp if you don't try."* Passives may not realize that their aggressive "friends" are manipulating them to do exactly what they want, so they blindly follow the herd.

"I'm starting to see why Passives and Aggressives end up working or living together."

Oh yes. They are a perfect match...well, perfectly destructive. Just think about the irony.

> **Passives do everything in their power to avoid hurt and anger, while Aggressives use hurt and anger to get their own way.**

It's a horribly unhealthy, twisted version of a win/win situation. Once it's clear that people are in the passive category— dedicated to meeting everyone else's needs but their own— they are prime targets for manipulation. Passives attract Aggressives. Professional manipulators see Passives as low-hanging fruit, ripe for the picking.

This explains why Aggressives love to work with, employ, be friends with, date, and marry Passives. The Passives play right into the Aggressives' hands and allow them to be in constant control.

FOR EXAMPLE:

Aggressive: *"Where do you want to go?"*

Passive: *"You choose. Anywhere is fine with me."*

Aggressive: *"Well, what do you want to do?"*

Passive: *"Oh, it doesn't make any difference. I'll enjoy doing whatever you want to do."*

That's the Aggressives' favorite answer! They want to choose. NO, they feel like they HAVE to choose. Not optional. On the flip side, Passives would rather let other people make the decisions so they don't feel responsible if things don't work out right. Too much pressure.

Passives want to avoid these kinds of conversations:

"Why in the world did you suggest this venue for the corporate kickoff? It's a disaster."

"I can't believe you recommended that restaurant! Horrible service."

"What a phenomenal waste of 2 hours...That tour was pointless. What were you thinking?"

No, thanks. Passives avoid taking responsibility for what to do or where to go because things could end in an angry confrontation. Or someone could be sad or disappointed. They would prefer to let others make the decisions rather than take a chance on being blamed if things go wrong.

People with dominant, passive personalities love to tell themselves that their input does not matter, so they might as well avoid the issue. Passives even make excuses when someone is treating them badly. Rather than place the blame on the aggressive manipulator, they often blame themselves saying, *"It must be me. Something I did must have caused this to happen."*

> ## No wonder Passives are such easy prey for Aggressives.

The Passive's fear of hurting someone or making them angry creates several ineffective strategies for dealing (or not dealing) with the world. For instance, the passive person usually has an almost pathological fear of expressing and being around anger. They start to feel the physical effects (headaches, stomach aches, anxiety, racing pulse) even when the most mundane irritations arise within or around them.

Passives usually feel most comfortable and at ease when everyone in their lives is happy and problem-free. Sure, that happens all the time, right? This explains why Passives prefer to deny reality and pretend to live in a cheerful, confrontation-free, Fantasyland world. That place doesn't exist. So Passives can pretend all they want, but they are often deeply unhappy on the inside.

Passives and Aggressives do seem to be magnetically

attracted. The manipulators and the manipulatable. Together, they create a very unhealthy relationship and a destructive pattern.

"What about passive behavior in the workplace?"

Sometimes it doesn't look like you might expect. Of course, it applies to the people who can't or won't make a decision. The ones who refuse to speak up and give their opinions. But it's also people who adopt a defeated attitude rather than creating a plan to change things and move forward.

I'm often surprised at conversations with people who recently lost their jobs through downsizing or a merger. Take my discussion with a currently unemployed man named Jackson, for example.

Connie: *"How long did you know that your job might be in jeopardy?"*

Jackson: *"We've all been worried about job security since the rumors started. About three months ago."*

Connie: *"So what have you been doing since that time?"*

Jackson: *"Uhhhh, what do you mean? What could I do? I just had to keep working every day as usual and wait to hear the news."*

Months have gone by. Time has been wasted. Talk about passively giving up control! It's like standing on the train tracks, watching the train as it comes toward you—and NOT MOVING OUT OF THE WAY.

WHAT?!?

Exactly. Assertives would have used that time to create an outstanding resumé, increase networking activities, and take classes to develop new skills. These actions would prepare them to find a new job if the worst should occur. That's not being disloyal to their current employers. It's smart and assertive!

I'm not suggesting people should search for jobs on company time. But they should be proactive about exploring new options. In fact, that's exactly what companies do. Organizations evaluate the competitive environment and frequently restructure (translation: firing and hiring) so they can best serve their customers and shareholders. It's assertive to be prepared for the future.

"In some ways, it seems like passive employees would be easier to manage."

Passive employees do appear to be awesome—at first. They seem to be positive and in agreement with everything that is going on around them. But deep down they lack both commitment and dependability. Because they struggle with saying no and setting boundaries, they can't be counted on to follow through. They are always overworked, overstressed, and overextended. They seldom take on leadership roles or initiate change. They are definitely risk-averse. Their strategy is designed to keep them safe and way, way under the radar. Out of trouble but disengaged.

Here's an example of a passive employee struggling to set boundaries and, consequently, paying the price.

The project manager gets requests from three different people who all need reports completed by 5:00. She realizes that she can't possibly meet the deadlines for all three of them, but she doesn't want to say no. That might disappoint them or make them angry. She reluctantly says yes, which prompts a massive headache and a knot in her stomach.

Of course, she fails. One report is completed on time, but not thoroughly. One is partially finished, but full of errors. The third one never makes it out of the original folder of notes. She is physically exhausted from trying to win a losing battle, and the same thoughts race through her mind over and over: *"It's not fair! Everyone takes advantage of me. Why do they treat me that way?"*

> **Passives like to blame everyone else for their plight, rather than take responsibility for the problem.**

The truth is, the project manager was unwilling to be assertive and tell people the truth. She wanted to be nice and avoid unpleasant feelings. But her attempt to be "nice" left others feeling angry and disappointed, while she felt guilty, inadequate, and flustered. In retrospect, the truth would have been much more pleasant.

If the passive project manager had taken an assertive approach, she could have handled it this way:

"You have each asked me for a report by 5:00. I'm guessing they would require nine hours of work total, and I only have six hours until the deadline. I could finish one today and complete the other two by tomorrow. Or we could pull in some extra help from another department and try to finish them all today. Which option would you like me to pursue?"

That response is assertive and polite at the same time. No meanness. No anger. Just an honest statement identifying the choices and consequences of each option. Assessing the situation and giving others the alternatives is far nicer than agreeing to do a job that can't and won't be done properly.

"If the passive person is in a management role, then what?"

Passive leaders, managers, and supervisors are certainly a problem, since they try to avoid any normal management functions that might lead to confrontation. They have difficulty delegating. They ignore tardiness and attendance problems. They accept reports turned in late. And they rationalize poor performance, behavior, and attitudes. They'd prefer to ignore the problems rather than deal with them.

Another issue? They often excuse their passive behavior by citing some of today's popular business buzzwords: *empowerment, shared leadership,* and *delegation.* Those words might seem like good explanations, but they should NOT involve abdicating authority and not doing their jobs. Struggling to set boundaries and failing to hold others accountable are not part of leadership "best practices."

Passive leaders are easily manipulated by aggressive employees, who delight in knowing they can get away with pretty much anything. But getting pushed around all the time is hard work. Passive managers always feel exhausted. They are overworked and overwhelmed. Needless to say, their teams aren't particularly productive or effective. Besides, passive leaders refuse to have the crucial conversations that can help employees to learn and grow. Everyone loses.

In my leadership sessions, I spend a great deal of time helping leaders work on their assertive negotiation skills. We focus on setting boundaries, giving clear directions, increasing employee engagement, and learning the strategies necessary to hold their employees accountable for their performance. Employees will, for the most part, model their attitudes and actions after the leaders in their companies.

I remind my leaders about this important principle:

> **Accountability sets boundaries for acceptable, appropriate behaviors within the workplace, and then it follows through with fair consequences for non-performance.**

Passive leaders shortchange everyone on the team. Assertive leaders take responsibility for creating healthy, functional teams that excel in their jobs.

{
REALITY CHECK

Passives invented the path of least resistance. Unfortunately, it's a dead-end street.

#cannotsayno   #GPSfail
}

SUMMARY
Points to Remember

1. Passives like to take the path of least resistance, avoiding problems and people rather than dealing with them.
2. Passives are easily intimidated and feel guilty if they try to say no or establish boundaries.
3. Passives sometimes feel so guilty that they take responsibility for others' problems and issues.
4. Everyone displays some level of passive behavior during their lives, perhaps in certain situations or with particular people.
5. Passives are highly intuitive and know how to sense others' needs and meet them without being asked. Unfortunately, they expect others to do the same (usually with great disappointment).
6. Passives learned this behavior through negative reinforcement (being afraid to speak out) or positive reinforcement (receiving praise for keeping quiet).
7. Passives are easy targets for Aggressives.
8. Compromising isn't passive, as long as both parties are getting something in return.
9. Shy people aren't necessarily passive; they might be thoughtfully listening and strategizing. The flip side is true, too. Outspoken people aren't necessarily aggressive.

10. Passives are more susceptible to peer pressure.
11. Passive behavior in business settings can be highly detrimental to team productivity, employee engagement, and performance.
12. Many times, Passives don't realize they have a choice to communicate in a different way.

chapter seven

DEALING WITH PASSIVES

If the difficult people in your life are NOT passive, you might be wondering why we even need to "deal with them." After all, Passives are the nice, saintly, never-cause-a-fuss, I-will-do-whatever-you-want people. Sounds pretty great, right?

WRONG.

The last chapter offered plenty of proof. Passives are usually considered nice people, but "nice without substance" can get old quickly. And to be honest, the "nice" Passives can end up being a real pain in the neck.

Many times, they:

- Refuse to be honest about what they are willing and able to do
- Allow themselves to become exhausted and overwhelmed
- Won't tell you how they really feel because they are too busy telling you what they think you want to hear
- Tend to be insincere and vague
- Avoid honest discussions
- Accept being less happy than they could be or want to be
- Bottle up their resentment until it overflows as anger

It's just not fun to work with or live with people who won't ever speak up. About anything. Choosing to ignore the problem would be easy—they can be effortlessly ignorable. But we'll definitely pay the price in the long term. And it's expensive.

> **If you manage, work with, date, live with, or socialize with a Passive, your sanity is at stake if you DON'T deal with it.**

Please. Read on. You'll thank me later.

"Is it even possible to help Passives become more assertive?"

Yes, it is. But don't assume it will be a quick process.

Remember, Passives learned to avoid confrontation over a long period of time. It would be highly ambitious to think we could transform them into secure, confident, tell-it-like-it-is people in one week.

Based on their past experiences, Passives don't trust us to respond positively to any assertive attempts they might make. They also usually lack the self-confidence needed to believe that their own needs and concerns are valid and worthy.

> ## Passive people are missing trust in themselves and confidence in others to stand up and be heard.

Interestingly enough, OUR problems with Passives are a perfect parallel. We don't trust that they will be honest when they share their feelings and concerns, and we lack confidence that they'll follow through and do what they say.

So back to basics.

We cannot change a passive person, but we can make sure that our behaviors and communication with them create an environment where they feel comfortable being assertive. When a passive person does make an attempt to be more open and honest, they need us to respond to their efforts with positive encouragement.

"So it's not fast, but it can happen. Where do I start?"

Passives need to experience what it is like to be assertive without making someone angry or hurting their feelings. If we truly want the Passives in our lives to shape up, then we have to commit to being assertive with them.

We must start by creating a manipulation-free zone. We need to avoid even the slightest hint of manipulation in our own behaviors and communications with the Passives. Then we need to help them understand that we WANT them to share their ideas, opinions, and concerns with us. We're INTERESTED in their thoughts, and we VALUE their perspectives.

From the other side, Passives need to feel completely safe to take that leap. No hidden agendas. No hurt or anger if they say or do something we don't like. No manipulation or retribution. We will NOT take advantage of them.

If you're now envisioning those famous team-building exercises with the trust falls, then you're getting the basic idea.

This is possible, but it's not easy. Passives are most likely surrounded by Aggressives in their lives, so building trust with them will take some time. And let's face it, you've got your own baggage. Your relationship with the passive person has been driving you crazy, so it will take some serious effort to mentally clean the slate.

> **If Passives even sense that you're still holding a grudge about a previous incident, they'll quickly retreat even further into their shells of insecurity. And you'll be back at square one.**

At work, the goal would be to create a space in which all employees feel like their opinions count. Encourage collaboration. Welcome diverse thinking. Make it clear that every PERSON has value. Every IDEA has value. That's the kind of environment that launches high-performance teams, and it's also the perfect safe zone to lure Passives out into the open. (Psssst...these folks are skittish. Don't make them feel like they're being ambushed.)

If Passives seem reticent to participate in meetings, focus on getting them more involved without making them feel cornered. When they do share an idea, let them know you appreciated their input. Or try approaching them away from the hustle and bustle of the entire team, and ask them to share their thoughts about a project. Be assertive with them. Over time, Passives will learn to adopt more assertive behavior.

"OK, so it's all about building trust."

Yes, but that's not as easy as it sounds. Building trust takes time, patience, and commitment. Plus, it's a two-way street. Getting someone to trust us can be a tough job. And, as I mentioned before, learning to trust someone who has kept quiet, refused to share, or lied to us to avoid confrontation of any kind takes even more effort.

The first thing you can do to develop trust with Passives is to **look within yourself.** Have you previously used manipulation (hurt or anger) in your relationships with the passive people

147

in your life? Have you taken advantage of them by using their passivity to get your own needs met?

Ask yourself if you ever say things like this:

"He won't mind taking on some extra work. He loves being busy."

"My boss doesn't care if I skip the weekly staff meeting. She totally covers for me."

"Let's have another beer. My wife loves to have time at home alone. She won't even notice I'm still gone."

These are all examples of taking advantage of someone and rationalizing that they really don't care. Guess what? They probably do care. But Passives give up and give in so quickly that we may not realize they are affected by our behaviors. Deep down, we all know we are extending our limits with another person, even if they don't speak up for themselves. We're pretending to believe that the Passives "won't mind," and the Passives are lying to themselves that this treatment doesn't matter.

"Whoa...are you really saying that Passives are liars?"

Well, basically, yes. And not just to other people. They have been lying to themselves for a long time. Not in a mean or malicious sense, but they are still dishonest. They continually cover up or ignore their own feelings and needs to avoid a hassle or to appease others. They avoid telling the truth if it might lead to an argument or confrontation.

If Passives feel tension levels getting high, they will say anything—or agree to almost anything—to get the situation back on an even keel. To us? That looks like a lie. A misguided attempt to deflect their real feelings. To Passives, it's a survival skill.

There it is again: this form of dishonesty can be traced right back to a basic lack of TRUST.

> **We cannot have healthy, successful, or happy relationships when we cannot trust others to tell us how they feel, what they need, what they want, what they are thinking, and what bothers them.**

"I get it. The goal is to help Passives be more open and truthful. Now what?"

Once you identify people who are predominantly passive, you want to consciously shift into direct, assertive mode. For example, the following conversation demonstrates how an assertive manager might interact with a passive employee. The manager knows from past experience that the employee would agree to anything to avoid disappointing her.

Manager: *"Katie, these two projects need to be finished today, and it's important for the numbers in both of them to be completely accurate. I need to know honestly whether you are comfortable with making that happen."*

Katie: *"If you need them, then I'll be glad to work on them."*

Manager: *"I know you're willing to help, but I need to know if you are totally confident that you can finish both projects in a short amount of time and still complete them as accurately as possible."*

Katie: *"Well, I'll most certainly try."*

Manager: *"I'm sure you'll try, Katie, but that isn't what I need to know. Are you positive that you can complete both projects accurately and on time?"*

Katie: *"Well, I don't really think I can do both as well as I would like unless..."*

Manager: *"Unless what?"*

Katie: *"Unless I have some help or stay late."*

Manager: *"Which of those would you prefer?"*

Katie: *"Well, my son has a playoff soccer game, and I'm supposed to drive tonight. But I guess I could..."*

Manager: *"Do you think staying late is the best option?"*

Katie: *"Not really. My son is counting on me."*

Manager: *"Then what else could you do?"*

Katie: *"I could ask Amy from the payroll department to help me for an hour. I know she has a light workload today."*

Manager: *"Great idea! Please give her a call and set that up. And tell your son good luck at his game!"*

Whew! Tiring, huh? But that's what you'll need to do initially to communicate with Passives and uncover their true feelings. No, not forever. Just until YOU establish a new level of trust, and THEY start to acquire some assertive skills. Hang in there! It will be worth the effort, I promise.

When we are rushed and busy, it's tempting to just accept the Passives' eager willingness to go along.

But we must always remember that Passives are wired to downplay or even cover up their real, honest feelings to keep the peace and please others. That's why it's critical to take the time to carefully word our requests for Passives so they genuinely understand:

- There are options for the process of complying with a request.
- We need them to be honest with us about their analysis of the options.
- They can trust us when they share their thoughts and feelings about the options.
- They can avoid conflict by resolving the issue now: discussing and selecting the best option, rather than dealing with the problems stemming from avoidance later.

Remember that you're helping the Passives to learn a new pattern of behavior. Your words, actions, and reactions are being carefully filed in those mental filing cabinets. Positive feedback is a major component of that training.

> Manager: *"Thanks so much, Katie. Nice work on the reports! I really appreciated your honesty about the process for completing both projects on time. Asking Amy to help was a smart move."*

Katie will soon realize that telling people what she truly needs does not, in fact, lead to an apocalypse. She files that information accordingly. Katie begins to feel safe that her manager won't get angry if she doesn't always say yes, and the manager can start to relax and trust that Katie will be honest. It's a beautiful thing.

"But what if the Passive who's driving me crazy is a good friend?"

It's the exact same frustration in a different setting. Conversations with a passive friend might sound like this:

> Julia: *"Hey, Kelsey! I have Saturday afternoon free. Want to go see a movie?"*
>
> Kelsey: *"Sure! That would be great."*
>
> Julia: *"What movie would you like to see?"*

Kelsey: *"Oh, I don't care. You pick one."*

Julia: *"I picked the last one. Why don't you choose this time?"*

Kelsey: *"Really, whatever you'd like to go see is fine with me."*

Julia: *"Well, I have been wanting to see that new romantic comedy. Does that sound good?"*

Kelsey: *"Of course, that's perfect! See you Saturday!"*

Here's the problem: that choice wasn't perfect. Kelsey would much rather see a drama or something with action, but she didn't feel comfortable speaking up. Maybe it's not very good. She would feel so embarrassed if she dragged Julia to a terrible movie. Better to avoid that potential awkwardness.

Kelsey is now feeling a bit resentful that she always ends up doing what Julia wants. It doesn't matter that Julia gave her every opportunity to weigh in on the decision and thinks Kelsey is totally on board.

If Julia begins to recognize Kelsey's passive tendencies, she can choose to change the conversation next time.

Julia: *"Hey, Kelsey! Want to go to the movies with me on Saturday afternoon?"*

Kelsey: *"Sure."*

Julia: *"What movie would you like to see?"*

Kelsey: *"Oh, I don't care. You pick one."*

Julia: *"Well, I'd enjoy seeing Movie A, B, or C. I've heard good things about all of them, so which of those sounds the best to you?"*

Kelsey: *"Really, I don't care."*

Julia: *"Well, you're my friend, and I like doing things you*

enjoy, too. I don't want to be the one who always
makes the decisions. So come on, friend...choose
a movie."

Kelsey: *"OK, I have heard some positive reviews about Movie*
A, but I don't really know for sure. You can't always
trust the critics. I don't want you to blame me if it
totally sucks."

Julia: *"Let's try that one! And I would never get mad at you*
if the movie sucks. If it's truly horrible, we'll just leave
and go have an early dinner. No big deal! Either way,
we'll get to spend some time together."

Passive people feel like they need our permission to provide their input and make decisions. They need to be reassured that it won't be the end of the world if they are wrong. We won't be angry or hurt. And they also need praise when they actually do speak up.

It's tough to have Passives in our personal lives. If they were our co-workers and we really couldn't stand the wishy-washiness, we could move to a different department or get a new job. But if we really value our friendships and want to maintain them, we have an even bigger incentive to change the dynamic of our relationships. Friends deserve to be treated assertively.

"OK, what if we have a child who appears to be naturally passive?"

154

> # Teaching children to be assertive is important. For them, it's a necessary life skill.

Adults can help children learn the techniques needed to face and deal with difficult times, people, and situations. These same skills could also possibly save their lives someday.

Let's never forget that the threat of giving in to peer pressure doesn't stop after adolescence for Passives. Many adults face the same situation in their businesses, community groups, social organizations, and even at home.

"That strategy is really questionable, and I don't feel right about it. But the rest of the team thinks it will be fine. I'll just vote to approve it."

"The last thing I want to do is volunteer for another committee. I'm hardly home with my kids as it is. But I just hate saying no, so I guess I can fit one more thing into my schedule."

"Another team happy hour after work? Seriously? I have to prepare for the meeting Friday. I guess I'll go and then stay up late to finish the presentation. I'm exhausted, but I don't want them to think I'm not being social."

Giving in to peer pressure is a real issue at any age, and the passive communication style is often the culprit.

The solution? As adults, we can demonstrate assertive behaviors with our colleagues and co-workers. They will experience positive reactions and solid results, which will give them an example of successful communication patterns.

For those of us who are parents, we have a responsibility to teach and model assertive communications to the children in our lives. When they gain a working knowledge of the different communication styles, they can make better choices. And when they understand the disadvantages of being passive, they can more quickly recognize the signs of peer pressure.

They'll be able to pinpoint difficult people who come into their lives: those who never learned to cooperate, don't respect those around them, and love to manipulate others to get their way. Instead, they'll recognize they have real choices when people are trying to manipulate or coerce them.

Becoming immune to peer pressure is a skill that will serve them well throughout their lives—making friends, dating, having roommates, maintaining long-term relationships, building successful careers.

ELIMINATING THE PASSIVE STYLE IS THE KEY.

"Frankly, this sounds exhausting. What if I'm not sure I really want the Passives in my life to change?"

Well, it will take patience and tact. A lot of it. And time. If you've ever been involved with teaching or coaching, you know that progress is often measured in inches, not miles.

The temptation to give up can be strong. The truth is, it's much more comfortable to maintain the status quo. Why change things if we're consistently getting our needs met in relationships and the Passives always do what we want? Aren't Passives actually kind of refreshing in this world of anger, rage, and short tempers? It really might be easier to have someone around who always goes along with the program. Sometimes it's hard NOT to take advantage of Passives; they're so darn easy.

That's your choice.

But before you give up, think about this. It's not really about whether you want to spend the extra time and effort to create a safe zone for the Passives in your life. It's about whether you want to get your own needs met in your relationships with them. Do you want to stay frustrated and disappointed when you can't count on them or don't know what they mean? Or need? Or want?

Yes, it will take all of your patience to adjust your relationships with the Passives in your life. But YOU will reap the benefits just as much as they do.

"I'm not really a patient person..."

So what happens if you give up? If you decide you can't spend 24/7 doling out assertiveness to the Passives in your life, you'll have to realize that the relationship may NOT survive for two reasons.

1. YOU CAN'T TAKE IT ANYMORE.

Passives generally become very exhausting and frustrating to interact with, and you may ultimately decide that it's too much trouble. Life is short.

The relationship might deteriorate after you find yourself screaming, *"But what do you want to do? Where do you want to go? Can't you ever offer a suggestion or have some input? Do you always have to be such a martyr?"* It's tough to have a relationship with someone who doesn't assertively participate, and it's hard to respect someone who lacks the confidence to speak up and tell you what they want, need, and feel.

"Sounds like Passives just don't get it."

Maybe they are too busy avoiding conflict. At some point, that may drive you crazy. For instance, conversations between respectful adults with opposing views can be interesting and educational. But not according to Passives. They view any type of interactions with disagreement as mean-spirited, angry, hostile arguments. Even when people are using calm tones and careful word choices. For Passives, disagreement is conflict— and they will avoid that at all costs. They simply don't realize that disagreements are a normal part of life.

If you value healthy debates, you may have to accept that the Passives in your life are not going to participate. Are you comfortable catering to that level of sensitivity? How long can you walk on eggshells? At some point, conflict avoidance actually creates conflict. Hello, Irony!

The other problem with Passives is that you never know where you truly stand with them. That vagueness can be enormously confusing for their friends, family, and colleagues. One of the advantages of a healthy relationship is knowing that the people you trust will be honest about how they feel. What they are thinking. What they need and want. Whether something is wrong. If the Passive always agrees no matter what, you are living in a vacuum with no barometer to measure the climate of the relationship. You might as well be living alone.

If you don't want to put in the effort to help adjust the Passives' behaviors, they can quickly change from "easy to get along with" to dull, monotonous, and totally frustrating.

If Passives are employees, you'll have to train them to be more assertive. Friends? Maybe they really aren't. At some point, you'll mentally decide you've had enough. More than enough. It's time to meet, hire, live with, be friends with, work for, and enjoy some new (assertive) people.

2. THEY CAN'T TAKE IT ANYMORE.

Communication styles aren't set in stone. Even hard-core Passives can eventually get pushed over the edge.

> **Passives are the ones most likely to have a "midlife crisis." Everything bottled up eventually explodes.**

If you don't work to help teach and guide Passives into more assertive behavior, they will keep bottling up the pressure of continually giving up and giving in. Unhappiness pushed inward. Dreams and wishes never fulfilled. Ideas never explored. Wants and desires compromised and never achieved. Years of built-up resentment may come streaming out in a momentary aggressive outburst.

They almost literally wake up one day and say, *"I AM DONE!"* And when Passives are finally done, they are DONE! In their minds, they tried everything they could to be a good person, help others, do the right thing, and please other people. And then, the lid blows off with an angry, bitter, I've-had-enough breakdown. Believe me, you don't want to be the target of the passive-overflow bomb.

This explosive response seems disproportionate to anyone who didn't realize the "passive pressure cooker" was reaching its limit. People respond with phrases like, *"Where did that come from? What's wrong? That's not like you at all! Settle down..."*

> # We complain when the Passives won't speak up; then we are surprised when they finally do.

In these situations, the Passives actually become aggressive. If they want to keep their aggression under wraps, they go for the passive-aggressive style: waging a secret war of manipulation.

(More on that in the chapters ahead!) Either way, the relationship is probably doomed.

"What if I try and nothing works? What if the Passive refuses to become more assertive?"

In that case, you have a choice to make about this relationship. Here are some specific suggestions:

IF THE PASSIVE IS YOUR
LEADER/MANAGER:

Your career may be suffering if you report to people who cannot give you clear direction, are always vague about policy, say what they think you want to hear rather than sticking to their beliefs, and refuse to support you if there's even a hint of confrontation. Is that where you really want to work?

In an age of mergers, layoffs, and downsizing, it's scary to have a passive boss who may be afraid to stand up for you, evaluate you fairly, fight for the raise you deserve, give you credit for your achievements, and help to remove the obstacles that get in your way. We need to believe our leaders will be our advocates if we work hard and deserve to be supported. Is it time to request a transfer to another department? Or spruce up your LinkedIn profile and launch a job search?

IF THE PASSIVE IS YOUR
EMPLOYEE:

You can't build a strong, successful team when some of the members cannot say no, are always overwhelmed, don't follow through, hide mistakes rather than dealing directly with problems, or can't effectively and assertively interact with co-workers and customers. Are these the people you want working for you? Or dealing with your customers or clients?

In a business environment where teamwork is essential, both leaders and employees must be able to trust their co-workers and count on them to do their part. If they fail to perform, it reflects poorly on you.

Sit down with the passive employees to discuss the situation. Let them know that their actions, behaviors, and performance are not where they need to be. If they can't make the required adjustments, they will need to consider a job assignment that works better with their style and personality. You want them to be successful, but your team might not be the right place for that to happen. Assertive and firm.

IF THE PASSIVE IS YOUR
PARTNER OR SIGNIFICANT OTHER:

You may be missing out on the best parts of a personal relationship if your significant other is emotionally closed off. If you're already providing a safe, assertive environment where your Passive feels comfortable sharing thoughts and explaining needs, then it's time for the cost/benefit analysis. How irritating or damaging is the passive behavior? Is it worth overlooking that?

If it's simply a matter of a Passive refusing to choose a place for lunch or a time to meet because this person truly doesn't care, then you can probably live with making most of the minor decisions in your relationship. However, if that passiveness is affecting you and your life because you can't count on your S.O., that's a different story. Do you want to continue on in a relationship where feelings, opinions, and ideas are NOT shared equally? It's your call. And it's a tough one.

It's difficult to justify severing a long-term relationship simply because someone has difficulty communicating openly. In many cases, Passives are pretty good at getting along and making a commitment to keep others around them happy. Unless that passivity is causing them to act in an unethical or illegal manner, it might be worth learning to love them, flaws and all. Focus on their many positive attributes, and do everything possible to create a trusting environment where they can feel safe being more open and intimate.

"I suppose it all comes back to being assertive, doesn't it?"

Exactly.

Passives thrive in the presence of assertive people. It's where they feel safe. And it's the only place where they find the courage to speak up.

Once trust has been established, Passives usually respond with enthusiasm to an environment that is free from manipulation. They have felt guilty, stressed, anxious, and afraid of confrontation for so long (and for so many reasons) that they often describe feeling "a sense of freedom for the first time" in their relationships with Assertives. At the office or at home. When Passives finally feel free to share their feelings, express their ideas, and get their needs met in a safe environment, it's liberating. Refreshing.

If you model assertive behavior long enough, the Passives in your life will begin to imitate your choices. And when you make it comfortable for them to give that style a try, amazing things can happen.

{

REALITY CHECK

Passives crave trust. Give them a manipulation-free zone, and you'll see a priceless change in your relationships.

#makeitsafe

}

SUMMARY
Action Plan: *Dealing with Passives*

1. Choose to assertively deal with the Passives who are driving you crazy if you want to have quality relationships and less stress in your life, both personally and professionally.

2. Fight the temptation to keep Passives in your life "as is" because they constantly let you have your way and ensure your needs will be met (usually before you ever ask).

3. Help Passives to become more assertive by creating a manipulation-free zone where they feel safe sharing their thoughts and opinions. Encouraging and rewarding their participation will begin to create a new tone for future interactions.

4. Take the time to genuinely listen to what Passives are saying, helping them to avoid making promises they can't keep. You may need to guide them through the process of analyzing the options available and making smarter choices.

5. Build greater trust with Passives, and you'll create the foundation for more open, truthful conversations.

6. Actively let Passives know that you value them, as well as their ideas and opinions.

7. Understand that helping Passives to become more assertive will require time and patience, but the relationship might not survive if you don't invest the effort. Either you'll reach a maximum level of frustration with their vagueness and non-participation, or they will "explode" from years of underlying resentment.

8. Ask for specific direction and feedback if you work for a passive leader. Polite, persistent requests will demonstrate your interest in their opinions. You want to ensure that their passivity doesn't block your career development and growth.

9. Gently coax passive employees to participate in team meetings or discussions. If they refuse to become more accountable, you'll need to determine if their personalities would be better suited for a different role.

10. Encourage passive friends and partners to be open with their feelings and opinions without any fear of retribution.

What if YOU might be the Passive?

1. Reflect on your past relationships and try to determine why you tend to use the passive style. Were you rewarded for it? Have you always taken the path of least resistance? Just remember that your past doesn't define your future. You can make a change!

2. Begin adopting the assertive communication style. Immediately. Today. Now. One sentence at a time.

3. Remind yourself that your thoughts, opinions, ideas, and feelings count. They really matter.

4. Recognize that other people can't read your mind. You can find ways to politely and gently express what you need without seeming like a bulldozer.

5. Learn to say no. If that seems inconceivable at first, look for optional responses that give you more control without using that "dreaded word."

   "Yes, I can do that. But I can't get started until tomorrow. Will that be OK?"

   "That won't work for me, but here are a few options you might consider..."

6. Make an effort to set limits and establish boundaries. Compromise is fine, but don't be a doormat.

7. Stop worrying, and smash the fear. It's not doing you any good. What's the worst that could happen if you speak up or change your behavior? What are the options? Could there be benefits?

8. Commit to dealing with tough issues NOW rather than ignoring them. Avoidance will likely make things much worse.
9. Don't take blame; take responsibility.
10. Find someone you trust who can help you practice expressing your emotions in a safe environment. It will get easier as you build up your confidence!

chapter eight

THE PASSIVE-AGGRESSIVE STYLE

Got people in your life who could win the gold medal in back-stabbing and revenge? Then I'm guessing you've already gained some hard-earned insights into the passive-aggressive personality.

I know, it's not pleasant. And they're usually experts at hiding their real feelings. When you finally figure them out, it could be too late.

There's a reason why great novels use Passive-Aggressives as the villains. They are truly sneaky. Devious. Underhanded. A winning plot definitely needs a Passive-Aggressive, but I'm guessing you'd prefer to NOT have one starring in your life. Am I right?

"Definitely not. But how can these people really be passive and aggressive at the same time?"

It does seem like a contradiction. We think of Aggressives as forceful and confrontational, while Passives are supposed to be laid-back and noncommittal. Amazingly, a passive-aggressive person manages to do both. Like a spiteful form of emotional multi-tasking.

EWWWWW.

Let me explain it a different way. Passive-Aggressives are the psychological equivalent of the Trojan horse: friends to your face, saboteurs behind your back. Out in the open, these individuals are remarkably friendly and kind. They may even pretend to be your best friends—the last people you'd ever expect to sabotage you.

But once they move in closer, they are often perfectly positioned to get away with mean (and cowardly) behavior. Mentally torturing you. Gossiping about you. Tattling on you. Turning others against you. Making you second-guess everything about the relationship. They're wholeheartedly addicted to the drama, and they want to direct the play.

These behaviors clearly represent the darker, greedier, and more devious part of the human personality.

Passive–Aggressives want to be in control without an obvious challenge, but the power struggle is very real.

They might be feeling angry, betrayed, jealous, threatened, or intimidated, but they will act as if everything is fine. (It most certainly is NOT!) It's all part of their deceptive strategy to make us suffer. We'll go along thinking that the relationship is fine, until we notice tiny clues that indicate problems are simmering below the surface.

A sarcastic tone. The guarded eye roll. Prolonged silence.

But what happens when we ask whether something's wrong? Total denial. That's the tough part.

Passive–Aggressives make us feel uncomfortable even questioning their integrity or commitment to the relationship. We might sincerely ask, *"Is something wrong? Is there a problem? What did you mean by that?"* They quickly smile and respond with, *"Who, me? No, I'm just fine. Nothing's wrong."*

Here's another answer you might recognize: *"That's not what I meant!"* or *"I was just kidding! What happened to your sense of humor?"* We hear the words, but we instinctively know there's some truth hidden behind the sarcasm. Sometimes not even hidden very well. The anger and hostility frequently peek out from behind the passive-aggressive mask.

This is exactly why Passive–Aggressives tend to love digital communications—emails, texts, Facebook posts, tweets. Those provide the perfect delivery system for ambivalent messages, completely stripped of the nonverbal cues that normally give recipients important context about emotion and intent. Was that a comment or a jab? A statement or a criticism? Is she implying this is my fault?

Without the benefit of a sarcasm font, we're left to stare at the raw words and make our own interpretations. Sure, we could speak up and ask for clarification. But that's almost guaranteed to generate denials, laced with hurt and disappointment that we could possibly doubt their motives.

Ughhh. Rock, meet hard place.

> ## When Passive-Aggressives communicate with a digital shield, anger and jealousy can fly right under the radar.

It's frustrating on every level, but delightfully convenient for them. If their goal was to drive us nuts, it's working.

"That's for sure! It seems like they are always trying to get the upper hand."

That's the understatement of the year. Passive-Aggressives are always keeping score. We might not even know we have an "account" with them, but they are recording every good deed they do for us. To them, there are no random acts of kindness.

You can bet they'll be referring to the account book the next time we try to assertively tell them no. After the dramatic expression of extreme hurt and the heavy sigh, they'll probably list everything they have ever done for us in the past. Oh, now we HAVE to help them. We OWE them.

"I hate it when people do that! It's so aggravating."

I agree. That's why the passive-aggressive communication style is most likely to destroy a relationship. It's hard to forgive and forget when people intentionally try to get their needs met at our expense—and do it in such a sneaky way that we don't even know what hit us. We are left feeling used and betrayed. There's no honest communication. No attempt to find a solution. And no easy way to break the cycle. Each person feels wronged, and each person is determined to wait for the other to apologize first.

Like the passive personality, Passive-Aggressives don't like face-to-face confrontations and avoid dealing with people assertively. Yet, like the Aggressives, they enjoy being in control and getting their own way. They are very comfortable using devious strategies to do just that. Also like the Aggressives, Passive-Aggressives are master manipulators, except they are much more subtle when using the tools of hurt and anger. In fact, they can be so subtle that you never suspect they are waging a secretive war with you at that very moment.

> **You know to keep your distance from Aggressives, but Passive-Aggressives lure you in and attack when you aren't even looking.**

"What kind of person uses passive-aggressive behavior?"

Most likely, we have all used passive-aggressive behavior in our relationships at one time or another, but the predominantly passive person is more likely to adopt passive-aggressive techniques. They can only exist in the whatever-you-want-is-fine realm for so long before the resentment overflows. We talked in the last few chapters about the potential for aggressive outbursts from Passives, but many times they choose to take their anger underground.

Their answer: manipulate *(aggressive)*, but do it so no one knows *(passive)*. They appear to give in and go along, but their passive-aggressive side may be working overtime to tip the scales back in their favor.

> **Passive-Aggressives believe their lives are controlled by others. They lack the skills and confidence necessary to be assertive. While they sense that outright aggression will get them into trouble, silent revenge is an attractive option.**

"Do all passive people end up being passive-aggressive?"

For the most part, yes. It's not normal or healthy for anyone to be controlled for long periods of time by another person in a relationship. As a species, we are blessed with the ability to reason and the opportunity to make choices based on that reasoning. We are not programmed to just go along passively, but rather to be independent and thoughtful.

When Passives find themselves in a manipulated and controlled environment where they are not allowed (or *perceive* that they are not allowed) to be an integral part of the relationship, they usually begin to experience some inner conflict. Those voices inside of them start whispering things like, *"You have a right to speak up," "This isn't fair,"* or *"What about YOUR feelings?"* Again, they have those same four choices.

- Learn to be more **assertive** so they can deal with their environment in a functional, healthy way.
- Continue to be **passive** and remain in a manipulative, controlled environment.
- Keep going until they finally "lose it" and become **aggressive**, choosing to match manipulation for manipulation.
- Plot to get even while continuing to go along in a **passive-aggressive** move.

The passive-aggressive choice seems like a way to maintain their usual demeanor while having the satisfaction of getting revenge. More often than not, this is the route they take.

Of course, we know that option's not going to end well. Unless they choose the **assertive** behavior, they are just destroying the relationship. Sooner or later. I'm betting sooner.

"Why don't Passive–Aggressives want us to know what they are doing or how they feel?"

Because we might use the assertive style on them. We might try to convince them to rationally and maturely solve the problem. To fix it. To end it.

COME ON, THAT RUINS ALL THE FUN!

If the conflict is resolved, our suffering is over. And making us suffer is part of their plan. They don't want to let us off the hook until they've exacted every ounce of revenge they feel we deserve.

Sick? You bet! Unprofessional? Totally!

> **Passive-Aggressives want difficult situations to go on indefinitely. Resolving issues is too easy. Their goal is to make us suffer, and they love to watch!**

Yes, there is a really disturbing side to this. Passive-Aggressives get an unhealthy enjoyment from the destructive payback process. They may even become hyper-focused on getting even with their victims because of the emotional satisfaction that provides.

"So do Passive-Aggressives ever get their needs met?"

Bad news, good news. Unfortunately, in the short-term, they often do. But in the long-term, rarely ever.

That's the whole, horrible irony about the passive-aggressive situation. In their blind passion to get even, not only do they fail to get their needs met, they usually end up hurting themselves in their quest for revenge. Plus, the reason behind their revenge—the issue that made them hateful and vindictive—is hardly ever dealt with or resolved. They end up further away from their goals. That's why this communication style is such a sad waste of time and energy.

I'm sure you've seen the passive-aggressive approach in action:

- **Co-workers who gossip, trying to establish their superiority and create a clique of supporters:** They lose the trust of everyone who hears their biting and inappropriate words.
- **Managers who take credit for others' ideas:** They lose the respect of everyone on the team.
- **Children who fail their classes to show their parents they are in control:** They end up spending their summers going to school rather than being with their friends.

- **Partners who withhold love and affection to teach the other person a lesson:** They miss out on the warmth and intimacy of a close relationship.

No one wins in those scenarios. It's tragic.

"Beyond tragic! So how can I identify the Passive-Aggressives in my life?"

Passive-Aggressives typically use four types of weapons (or a creative combination). Some are used more in business settings, and some are used more in personal settings. I think you'll recognize ALL of them.

- **Gossip:** sharing information (not necessarily true) as a way to hurt others
- **Tattling:** reporting someone to authorities for wrongdoing that may or may not be legitimate
- **Silence:** using the silent treatment to create stress and concern in others
- **Traps:** setting someone up to create a valid reason for getting angry with them later

Let's take a deeper dive on each one of these.

1. GOSSIP

When I'm asked to speak to large organizations about team building—*believe it or not*—I include an entire segment on gossiping. That might initially sound like a presentation for third graders, but you'd be shocked by the reality. This passive-aggressive behavior can literally destroy a department or a team. I've seen it over and over. It happens in companies of every size and in every industry.

> ## Far beyond creating hurt feelings on the playground, gossiping can pack a powerful punch in the corporate world.

Low morale. High employee turnover. Lost productivity. Failed businesses.

"All of that from gossip? Crazy..."

No kidding! It's a serious problem, and it's perpetrated by passive-aggressive people: those who thrive on "getting the dirt" about others and selectively sharing it to demonstrate their superiority. But the gossips aren't in it alone. These Passive-Aggressives unknowingly make you a partner in crime.

"I accidentally overheard Stan saying that Kelly will probably get fired. She screwed up big-time."

"I got a glimpse of the confidential report, and you'll never guess how much money he makes."

"Ethan and Marina just got back from another business trip. Uh-huh, I swear something's going on there."

You may not like the stories they are spreading, but your lack of response (or just the fact you hang around to hear the latest scoop) tells gossipers that you agree with every word. They honestly don't care if you add to the stories or just stand there and listen. It's all the same to them. But there are no outside observers. If you don't object to the gossip, you're quietly condoning.

2. TATTLING

Tattlers are constantly complaining about others' actions or reporting their "bad" behavior to an authority figure (regardless of whether the infractions are valid). Their sole intent is to hurt people: to harm others' reputations by sharing information that isn't vital.

And isn't there just something about the word "tattling" that implies whining? My thoughts exactly.

> **Passive-aggressive tattlers enjoy the sense of power they feel from reporting a supposed violation and watching someone else get in trouble.**

What better way to get payback on someone who has caused them pain or shame or embarrassment? If you hurt me, I'll even the score—and I'll get someone else to do the dirty work.

"I've heard that Nathan's clients don't really like him. Just thought you should know."

"It's none of my business, but Sara has been leaving early. Probably no big deal, but wanted to keep you in the loop."

"Ummmm...I hate to bring this up, but Troy really isn't ready for Friday's presentation. Would you like me to help him?"

Any truth there? Maybe, maybe not. Doesn't matter; suspicion is brewing. Their mission is accomplished. If tattlers are anything, they are experts at stirring the pot.

"Are there any times when tattling is warranted?"

Yes. There ARE legitimate reasons to report certain behaviors to a higher authority without being labeled a tattler. If a person is doing something illegal, unethical, or slanderous, you have a responsibility to speak up. Or if you've had one-on-one conversations with a superior about resolving a situation that isn't changing, that's fair game too. Sometimes you have no choice but to get help from a senior leader. (More details on that in the next chapter.)

3. SILENCE

Sometimes silence speaks volumes. I think it would be safe to say that we've ALL been on both sides of the silent treatment.

When Passive-Aggressives want to really get under our skin, they clam up and watch us squirm. We don't know what they're doing or thinking or silently plotting. And we want to know! NOW! The silence makes us feel uncomfortable, insecure, and downright worried. When we ask if something's wrong, they look at us innocently and deny the existence of any problems. And that makes us even crazier. Of course, something is wrong. They just don't want us to know.

AHHHHHH, MANIPULATION 101.

That puts the Passive-Aggressives firmly in control, right where they want to be.

We've all probably seen this tactic used at work and at home. The problem is, it's an unhealthy way to resolve problems. We can't repair a relationship by refusing to speak. It's not logical.

> **Passive-aggressive behavior is all about control. Who is going to give in first? The need for power overrides everything, even at the risk of destroying the relationship.**

If both people are fairly stubborn, the silent treatment can continue for a long time with each person perceiving themselves as the innocent victim, waiting in vain for the other person to give in and apologize. Not a productive strategy, to say the least.

Speaking of unproductive, the silent treatment in business can wreak major havoc. Angry professionals who aren't speaking to their co-workers don't share information that is vital for implementing key initiatives. They conveniently forget to copy someone on the group message with the link to the webinar. Or they sit silently in a brainstorming session refusing to participate and reducing the quality of new ideas. When communication shuts down, performance takes a hit.

"Do men and women use the weapon of silence differently?"

Sometimes I do see a gender difference in the use of silence as a passive-aggressive behavior. Most of us pay people back by doing to them exactly what we would HATE for them to do to us. That's why women tend to use the silent treatment as a form of punishment more than men.

Many women (not all, of course) can't stand it when people appear angry and refuse to speak to them. It worries them. Concerns them. Stresses them. They are afraid they've hurt someone's feelings or made another person angry. They want to know what they said or did that could be responsible for the silence. In those cases, they will do almost anything to get the other person to speak to them again.

In personal relationships, some women mistakenly believe

that giving the silent treatment is a punishment—one that will bother men just as much as it bothers them.

You already know where this one's going, don't you?

Surprise! Most men don't view the silent treatment as a form of punishment. In fact, it typically takes them about an hour to realize we've even stopped talking to them. Ha! For many men, the silent treatment is actually viewed as a reward!

I've confirmed this theory in my therapy sessions with a wide range of men. If they picked a fight early Sunday morning and their wives used the silent treatment in response, that meant the guys could watch football games all afternoon without interruption. For a sports enthusiast, that's the greatest gift ever!

"Honey, the Cowboys are playing the Packers next Sunday. Could you make plans to punish me with that silence thing again?"

Yeah, sometimes those attempts to get revenge can backfire. With that said, plenty of men have figured out how to use the silent treatment for their own advantage. They also enjoy the power of forcing everyone else to wonder what they are thinking. It's a strategy that frequently works on employees, bosses, partners, even friends. Cue the churning anxiety. Are they angry? Looking for a new job? Getting ready to fire me? Cheating? Filing for divorce? Passive-Aggressives can sense the mental twisting and turning they prompted, and that sense of control can make them almost giddy.

4. TRAPS

If you've ever felt like the difficult people in your life were setting you up, you were probably right. They were baiting you. Luring you into a trap. No, that was NOT your imagination.

Oh yeah, that happens all the time.

> ## Set-ups are a huge part of the Passive-Aggressive's arsenal of vindictive weapons.

For whatever reason, Passive-Aggressives get ticked off at a real or imagined "offense"—something that was done or not done. So to get back at the people who made them angry, they deviously create a situation that will cast themselves in the role of the victim. That gives them a legitimate reason (in their own minds) to lash out, and they'll do whatever they can to make the other people look bad or feel bad. Or some of each.

Here's an example.

Shannon was upset when her manager picked George to make the client presentation on behalf of the team. It wasn't in her nature to complain about the choice, but she knew she was much more knowledgeable about the products than anyone else in the group. Besides, in her view, George had been very pushy about wanting the position. Almost lobbying for it. She didn't say a word, but she definitely felt slighted.

Shannon waited until the last minute to provide George

with the charts he needed, which created a time crunch. On the day of the presentation, George grabbed the final report from the printer and raced out the door to the client's office. Shannon had noticed the "out of paper" message but, once again, didn't say a word. When George got to the big meeting, he was flustered when he realized his report was incomplete. He looked disorganized and unprepared, which prompted complaints from the client to Shannon's manager. According to Shannon, that was a fair consequence for the bad decision of choosing George over her.

Of course, putting the client relationship in jeopardy prompted a surge in stress and overtime for everyone on the team as they worked to regain trust and confidence.

This same type of passive-aggressive trap-setting can also happen on a personal level.

Tony and Anna have been married for ten years. Despite Tony's many great qualities, he never seems to remember Anna's birthday. He adores Anna, but tracking birthdays is just not his thing.

If Anna took the assertive approach here, she would say:

"By the way, Saturday is my birthday. I'd love to have dinner somewhere romantic. I'll even make the reservations..."

> # Wow! Tell someone exactly what you need, and you might just get it.

On Saturday evening, Anna could be sitting in an expensive restaurant having a memorable birthday celebration.

Or she could go with the passive-aggressive option. Anna could test Tony to see if he really loves her. She could set him up by not mentioning her birthday and waiting to see what happens. Unfortunately, Anna is setting herself up, too. For major disappointment. If history is any indication, Tony will NOT remember her birthday, so Anna will spend the day acting hurt and playing the victim nobody loves.

This was definitely a trap. Anna was looking for a reason to play the part of the unloved wife, and she knew exactly how to make that happen.

When Passive-Aggressives attempt to hurt others, they always end up hurting themselves as well.

"It seems like passive-aggressive behavior shows up a lot in our personal lives."

Correct. Personal relationships can be highly emotional. That creates fertile ground for tiny irritations to slowly grow, turning into the potential for knock-down, drag-out arguments. When it comes to family members, significant others, partners, children, parents, and close friends, we're fully invested. These represent long-term connections in our lives that come with the pressure of no easy exit strategy (unless an attorney is involved).

Jobs come and go; family is forever.

Even when we know the benefits of using the assertive style at work, that concept sometimes goes out the window once we get home. We're tired and cranky. We expect our families to understand and cut us some slack. Maybe even coddle us a little.

It's sad to think that we save our worst attitudes and behaviors for the ones we love the most. But, as you probably know, this happens all the time. With major consequences.

Family members can only console and tolerate the grumpy ones for so long before passive-aggressive behavior sneaks in. Then they match that grumpy and raise it with some bitterness. Or one person is constantly distracted, and the other feels neglected—and eventually begins to return the favor. Give them some of their own medicine!

> ## The passive-aggressive payback loop can become fierce. And last for years.

Most marriages and long-term relationships can overcome some isolated incidences of passive-aggressive behavior. But when that becomes the style of choice, things start to fall apart. Next to abuse and addiction, passive-aggressive behavior is the most destructive thing in a marriage. Deceit, secrecy, and a desire for revenge replace trust, sharing, and openness. Selfless feelings become selfish. Instead of thinking of what you can do for the other person, you are thinking about what they haven't done or what they've done wrong. Are they in control? Or being controlled? What's the score?

Passive-aggressive behavior can destroy relationships like nothing else can.

"If that's true, why do people continue to use it? Are they doing that on purpose?"

Yes and no. Unfortunately, so much of what any of us do and say is done without thinking: we just react. So some passive-aggressiveness may occur without premeditation—simply as a reaction to behavior we don't like or appreciate.

Occasionally, plenty of people from all communication styles have actively chosen to use the passive-aggressive approach in their lives. They temporarily applied the silent treatment or decided to set someone up. It was intentional, but it was a limited-use application.

On the other hand, genuine Passive-Aggressives deliberately choose this behavior. It's a habit, a way of life. In fact, they may invest considerable time thinking about what can be done to even things up on their mental scoreboard. They plan it all out, and they feel totally justified using revenge tactics. They believe they have been mistreated and have a right to get even.

The problem is that passive-aggressive behavior never evens the score, and both sides still lose. They seldom feel sorry for how they treat others. Eventually, neither person has any desire to be cooperative, compassionate, or loving. It's the point of no return. The relationship is likely damaged beyond repair.

> **It's very hard to feel love or respect for people while you are constantly thinking of ways to hurt, punish, or pay them back. Especially if they are thinking the same things about you!**

This is why assertive communication is so important in jobs, long-term relationships, friendships, marriages, parenting, and leadership. There must be a commitment to share feelings and concerns openly and honestly so passive-aggressive behavior can be avoided.

{
REALITY CHECK

Passive–Aggressives: victims or villains?
They deliver sabotage with a smile.
And you never see it coming.

#therevengeisreal
}

SUMMARY
Points to Remember

1. Passive-Aggressives feel like victims *(passive),* but they set out to pay people back for the real or perceived injustices *(aggressive).*
2. Passive-aggressive behavior destroys trust and relationships through the use of sabotage and subterfuge.
3. It's difficult to identify Passive-Aggressives, because they are usually kind to our faces and unkind behind our backs.
4. Passive-Aggressives silently keep score of the good deeds they've done for us so they can demand payback at a later time.
5. Passive people frequently adopt passive-aggressive behavior when they are tired of giving in but lack the confidence to be assertive.
6. Passive-Aggressives don't want us to know how they feel so they can launch a sneak attack that will catch us off-guard.
7. Passive-Aggressives believe they have a right to get even, which justifies their revenge tactics.
8. They typically use four weapons to get back at others: Gossip, Tattling, Silence, and Traps.
9. Passive-Aggressives usually end up hurting themselves in their pursuit to hurt others.

10. Passive-Aggressives in the workplace create a toxic environment that tears apart teams and pits co-workers against each other.
11. In our personal lives, passive-aggressive behavior can erode relationships with family members and friends who suffer in the climate of deceit and betrayal.

chapter
nine

DEALING WITH PASSIVE-AGGRESSIVES

It's tough to win a battle you don't realize you're fighting.

Passive-Aggressives are so sneaky and insidious that they will almost make you thankful to have a few Aggressives in your life. *(Wow. Contemplate that thought for a moment.)* At least with the overt manipulators, you know who and what you are dealing with—and that gives you some options. You can take strategic action to make it a fair fight.

But with Passive-Aggressives, you don't recognize the opponent. You don't even realize you're on the battlefield until, suddenly, you're in the line of fire. Absolutely no warning.

Passive-Aggressives are like snipers hidden in trees. Dealing with them may be the toughest challenge of all.

"Yeah, I'd prefer to avoid those people altogether."

That's understandable. The first lesson in dealing with passive-aggressives is to **be aware that these behaviors exist in the world.** Not that you should be suspicious of every person who wants to be your friend, but it's smart to watch for potential signs in an effort to protect yourself.

Your personal and private information can be extremely dangerous in the hands of Passive-Aggressives. It's a frightening thought, but anything you tell a Passive-Aggressive can and will be used against you. Not today perhaps, but sometime in the future when you are more vulnerable.

On numerous occasions, I've coached people who opened up to a co-worker with their innermost feelings, only to discover later that the confidential information was used against them. It's a horrifying realization and a painful breach of trust. Just be selective when you choose to share your secrets, fears, and weaknesses.

DON'T BE PARANOID; JUST PAY ATTENTION.

"Scary. But good to know...Now what?"

In any situation where you suspect passive-aggressive behavior, you must begin by taking a close look at your own communication style first. This is definitely not meant to accuse you of the problem or excuse the Passive-Aggressives. Their behavior is still unhealthy, nonproductive, and even hateful. But remember the guiding principles you've learned about relationships throughout this book:

> **We play an integral part in how people treat us. We can change ourselves, but we cannot change others.**

I know what you're thinking. This really would be so much easier if we could just change other people. I agree.

Back to reality.

Ask yourself honestly if your own behavior could possibly be contributing to an environment that allows Passive-Aggressives to thrive. For people to be motivated to seek revenge, they must first identify what appears to be (in their own minds) an injustice done to them.

Passive-Aggressives are reacting to what they believe was inappropriate, unacceptable, unfair, or unjust treatment. That doesn't necessarily mean you did anything wrong. But in some cases, maybe you did. Accidentally or not. Either way, the Passive-Aggressives are all about getting payback to even the score. Covertly and deviously. When you're least expecting it.

After being on the receiving end of a sneak attack, your first response probably won't be to "hug it out." Or even "talk it out." Understandable. But let your guard down a bit, and try to answer these questions.

- Have you legitimately hurt or offended the Passive-Aggressives in any way (recently or in the past)?
- Have you said or done something that they could possibly perceive in a negative light, even if it was unintentional?
- Have you picked up on any clues that might signal their anger or irritation?
- How did you respond to those?

It's uncomfortable to think of your own words or actions as being the catalyst for your subsequent suffering, but this does give you a starting point to understand the Passive-Aggressives' behaviors on the way to diffusing them. If you can assertively discuss the issues and clear up any misunderstandings (or apologize!), you may be able to start improving the relationship's negative vibe. Baby steps, perhaps, but at least you're moving forward!

All that being said, you might not deserve ANY of the blame. There's a fair chance that you did absolutely nothing wrong to provoke them. Passive-Aggressives simply tend to rank higher on the jealousy scale. They see what others have, and they want it. Jealousy becomes anger. And anger fuels sabotage.

> **Passive-Aggressives are quick to perceive others who have "more" as a threat to their own careers, relationships, and lives. They see the world through the lens of scarcity rather than abundance.**

"OK, I know about the Passive-Aggressive weapons. How do I disarm them?"

Good question. Let's cut to the chase.

At this point in the book, I'm confident you can now guess the top strategy for dealing with Passive-Aggressives. Go ahead, guess. Now please tell me you enthusiastically chimed in with some form of answer that involved assertive communications. You did, didn't you? Nice work!

> **If you're on a Passive-Aggressive's radar, don't react by getting angry. Don't give in. Get assertive! That's the ONLY strategy that can improve your relationships and reduce your stress.**

Without someone to model assertive behavior for Passive-Aggressives and the people around them, every interaction may become an opportunity for revenge. Remember: returning the payback punch isn't going to help us get ahead in life. It's not our place in the cosmic scheme of things to teach others their lessons by using behavior as bad as their own. Instead, it's our responsibility to demonstrate what sane, healthy, assertive communications look and sound like.

WHAT TO DO ABOUT GOSSIP

The obvious solution to curb the passive-aggressive behavior of gossiping is to take a stand against it. Right? Well, it's not that easy. Here are several reasons why:

- Many people actually enjoy a bit of gossip. They like being an "insider" and having access to exclusive information. The juicier, the better. Plus, hearing about others' mistakes and misfortunes makes them feel better about themselves.

  "Glad I'm not in her shoes!"

- People are afraid that standing up to the gossipers will make them the next victims. They'd rather participate (actively or silently) than become the subject of future gossip.

  "What if they start talking about me next?"

> **When it comes to gossip, the Passive-Aggressives leave you in a bizarre, I-need-to-stop-this-but-I-can't-risk-stopping-this paralysis. For them, that's paradise.**

No matter what you say or do, the gossip WILL be about YOU at some point. It's inevitable, so let go of the *"what if"* anxiety. And stop worrying about offending gossipers by speaking out and telling them you'd prefer not to talk about other people. Your own self-respect is much more important, so do what's right and refuse to participate or even listen. Be brave and speak up on behalf of someone who is being targeted by gossipers; perhaps someone else will defend you when the time comes.

"I'm not comfortable with this conversation; please excuse me."

"I don't believe there's any validity to those claims. I prefer to give people the benefit of the doubt and wait to get the actual facts."

"Wyatt couldn't have been screaming at Andrew in the conference room last week; he was on a business trip in New Zealand."

"But what if senior leaders are actually participating in the gossip?"

It happens. In some companies, gossip is used as a way of disseminating information—leaking it and monitoring reactions before making formal announcements. That provides an opportunity to adjust any details that were poorly received. But in the meantime, everyone in the office is filled with stress and panic and dread. Short-term gain, long-term disaster.

Your response depends on your position within the company. If you're a decision-maker, take action to shut it down. If you're not, assertively discuss the unintended effects with someone who has the power to make a change. It's in the best interest of the company (and the bottom line) to operate from a truthful, honest place.

WHAT TO DO ABOUT TATTLING

Sometimes passive-aggressive tattlers in the office are lone wolves; other times an entire organization perpetuates the problem. Before you can change the negative impact of tattlers, you'll need to identify the source and determine the scope of the problem.

Is there a single person who repeatedly tattles on others in your company? What's driving that behavior? Does your corporate culture seem to allow tattling? Worse yet, enable it? Or encourage it? Some companies actually accept the responsibility for following up on every tattlers' gripes and complaints. The climate of suspicion becomes toxic in the corporate courtroom, where "innocent until proven guilty" doesn't apply.

Whether you're dealing with an individual or an epidemic of passive-aggressive tattling, it might be helpful to establish some ground rules to help you minimize the problem:

- Tattling without merit should NOT exist in a healthy, functional workplace.
- It is NOT your responsibility to listen to tattlers whose main intent is getting someone in trouble.

- It is NOT your responsibility to fix the tattlers' problems if they haven't even tried resolving them on their own.
- It IS your responsibility to model assertive communication skills for tattlers so they can learn to resolve their own problems face-to-face with other people.

As with most things in life, some exceptions apply.

Here are three valid reasons why an employee should report another one to management: if someone is doing something...

- Illegal
- Unethical
- Dangerous

Those situations are NOT considered the passive-aggressive form of tattling. Instead, employees have a RESPONSIBILITY to share that knowledge with people who can swiftly resolve the issues.

Another legitimate reason for employees to share information about others' actions is when seeking guidance from managers or authority figures. When the intent of the conversations is to improve their own skills, support their teams, clarify false statements, or work through difficult issues one-on-one, those situations don't qualify as tattling. Those are collaborative discussions with positive goals.

As you can see, tattling is not exactly a cut-and-dried offense. When in doubt, look for the intentions. Those will help you determine whether you are dealing with a report or revenge.

"OK, how do I create an environment that minimizes tattling?"

The goal is to transform a dysfunctional tattling environment into an assertive, open, and collaborative one. Leaders need to set the tone. Here's an example.

Lorenzo: *"I wanted to talk to you about Nick."*

Manager: *"Sure!"*

Lorenzo: *"I'm having a problem with him. He always..."*

Manager: *"Wait a minute. Did Nick do anything illegal, unethical, or dangerous?"*

Lorenzo: *"Well, no..."*

Manager: *"OK, what did Nick say when you discussed the problem with him?"*

Lorenzo: *"Umm...I haven't actually mentioned this to him yet."*

Manager: *"Why not?"*

Lorenzo: *"I thought that's something you would do...as the department manager."*

Manager: *"No, Lorenzo. That's your responsibility. But I can help you approach that conversation with him in a more assertive way."*

Lorenzo: *"Oh...I couldn't...no..."*

Manager: *"Yes, you can! I know you can do this. Think for a moment. Why don't you want to discuss this issue directly with Nick? What's holding you back?"*

Lorenzo: *"I'm not really sure."*

Manager: *"Well, what would happen if you met with him and talked through the problem face-to-face? How could you explain your concerns to him in a way that generates a positive solution instead of just doling out judgment or criticism? I can help you figure that out. I'm here to support you in resolving your own conflicts."*

Assertive managers don't jump in to rescue everyone in a difficult situation. They guide others to confidently solve problems and resolve conflicts on their own.

If Lorenzo doesn't seem willing to take responsibility for the problem after that discussion, the manager can offer to have Nick join them in the office to begin working out the solution. Two results are possible. The manager can mediate the discussion. Or Lorenzo will be highly motivated to confront Nick on his own. Either way, Lorenzo will think twice before complaining about people to his manager without confronting them directly first.

Unhealthy, passive-aggressive tattling can be stopped if management refuses to participate in the process. I always remind leaders that it is IMPOSSIBLE to have a team that works together effectively if tattling is allowed. Or worse yet, encouraged.

Teams need to trust one another—and trust cannot exist in an environment where employees must worry about whether others are talking behind their backs and tattling about them to their bosses.

"What about tattling within my family? My kids might already be experts."

If tattling is happening at home with your children, you already know the answer. Be an assertive parent, and make tattling unacceptable. The same rules apply—with the same caveat about speaking up in potentially dangerous situations. Model assertiveness. Teach them assertive behavior and responses. Help them learn to identify the non-assertive styles and some strategies to deal with people who use them.

Just think of how successful that could make them, using assertiveness throughout their school years and moving on to their lives as adults. They can enter the business world with confidence and integrity, giving their careers an enormous boost. They'll have the capacity to create friendships that last a lifetime. They'll have the tools to develop solid, loving, long-term relationships. And at some point, they'll teach their own children how to navigate in a world that could certainly use a lot more openness, honesty, and trust.

**Invest the time and effort to help your children become assertive.
Best ROI you'll ever get.**

Parent of the Year award? I vote yes.

WHAT TO DO ABOUT THE SILENT TREATMENT

When people give you the silent treatment, your only hope of drawing out a discussion about the problem is to be assertive. If you ignore it, nothing changes. If you get angry, they have succeeded at pushing your buttons. Nothing changes. If you sulk and get your feelings hurt? Again, nothing changes.

At the office, you'll need to gather the courage to have a calm, professional, assertive conversation with the Passive-Aggressives who are refusing to interact. If you're in a position of authority, you may have to explain that their behaviors need to change or they will be jeopardizing their employment. Corporate settings are NOT the place for childish actions like the silent treatment. That type of behavior can have a negative impact on colleagues and customers, and it could undermine the organization's ability to reach serious goals.

"What about at home?"

> ## In terms of personal relationships, the silent treatment is one of the oldest (and least effective) strategies used by those who have a problem with their partners or significant others.

So what if you are the one getting frozen out by the silence?

First, tell the other person that you recognize their attempts to get even with you for some perceived injustice (and it may be a very real injustice).

"OK, it is apparent that you aren't speaking to me for some reason. If you are upset or angry with me, I have no way to understand what I did unless you tell me. And if I don't know why you're upset, we can't work on fixing the problem. I really care about you, and I want to make things better. So when you are ready to resolve the problem, let me know."

That's a strong, assertive statement! But, let's be realistic, the Passive-Aggressives are not likely to start spilling out their emotions and feelings after one attempt. If your mature plea is met with more silence, you can always follow that up with something like this:

"Refusing to speak to me won't help us figure this out, but I realize I can't make you talk. So, I'm going to finish this project and have some lunch. Maybe go the park. I'll wait until you are ready to discuss the situation with me."

Then, do just that. Go about your normal routine, and let them sulk until they decide to deal with the problem in a more mature, assertive way. Don't let the silent treatment work on you! Teach them that you will be fine while they are not speaking. You're perfectly willing to wait until they decide to grow up and communicate assertively.

"I thought we weren't supposed to ignore negative behavior."

Well, that is true except in the case of the silent treatment—for two reasons.

First, we should never ignore behavior that is inappropriate, unacceptable, unethical, or illegal. The silent treatment doesn't fall into those categories. The Passive-Aggressives are just being childish by pouting and refusing to speak. They want you to play the lead in their drama; don't audition for that part.

Second, ignoring their silent treatment is exactly what the Passive-Aggressives cannot stand. They are dying for you to respond with a reaction: ANY reaction will do. Concern, frustration, irritation, worry, fear, anger. Take your pick. NOT reacting drives them crazy—and it's your best strategy to get them talking again.

One thing to clarify.

> # Ignoring the silent treatment does NOT mean matching their behavior by refusing to speak to them.

Giving the silent treatment back just results in those icy, terrible phases where neither person speaks for days or weeks. That is simply double manipulation. If you resort to the passive-aggressive silent treatment, they win. They irritated you so much that you chose to engage in immature behavior, too.

Instead, follow my suggestion. Go on with your normal day and act as though nothing is wrong.

Picture a situation where a mother has put a child into time-out. The little boy stands in the corner with his arms folded, huffing and puffing, with a look that says, *"You are so mean, and I'm never going to forgive you for punishing me!"* What does Mom do? She goes about her business, fixing dinner or reading a book. She uses assertiveness to put the child in time-out, and now she uses assertiveness to ignore his "attitude." Pretty soon, the boy becomes exhausted from maintaining his angry look and aggressive stance.

By the way, that same technique works with co-workers, team members, employees, partners, and friends. The Passive-Aggressive's silent treatment is only effective when the other person can't stand the silence and chooses to give in and react.

WHAT TO DO ABOUT TRAPS

If the difficult Passive-Aggressives in your life (professionally and personally) tend to set you up for an angry outburst or a shamefully sullen response, there are several steps you can take to deal with the pattern of emotional traps.

1. Pay closer attention to identify signs of trap-setting, especially if that's been an ongoing issue in your relationships at work or at home. Listen carefully and watch for nonverbal cues. Is there a tone or attitude that indicates something else going on below the surface?
2. If you miss the signs and end up with a confrontation from an angry Passive-Aggressive, let tempers die down before talking about the situation. Then have a calm, assertive discussion to let the person know that you are concerned about the underlying emotions that might be causing this behavior.
3. Try to create a collaborative environment for finding solutions—new patterns of behavior for both of you that will result in win/win solutions.

"I know you're angry with me because I didn't turn in the paperwork by 5:00 yesterday. I realize that's a problem, and I apologize. I noticed that I wasn't copied on the email from you with the updated deadline. I understand keeping the project on track is very important to you...what steps could we take to make sure I remain in the loop so I can do my part?"

"What other tactics can I use to get better results when dealing with Passive-Aggressives at work?"

Be intentional about your words and actions. Passive-Aggressives are trying to get a reaction; don't give it to them. Your goal is to be calm, confident, and collaborative.

Let's look at another example. During a staff meeting, you are presenting new ideas to the entire department. One employee named Alex sighs heavily, folds his arms, rolls his eyes, and makes snide comments to the person next to him. He isn't keeping his feelings to himself, but he's not angrily attacking you or the idea. Alex has chosen to be passive-aggressive, making his feelings known without addressing the issue.

First, stay calm. If you aggressively confront Alex, there could be an ugly scene. Using aggression to fight a Passive-Aggressive will set the stage for a major power struggle.

Second, remain confident that you CAN address this issue. If you ignore Alex, his behavior will get worse. Plus, the people around Alex may get the idea that snarky looks or comments are acceptable and even "cool."

Third, think collaboratively. Despite the fact that Alex is acting like a 4-year-old, could he actually have a valid objection to your idea? Did he identify a hidden risk you don't see? Demonstrate that you are open-minded and mature, welcoming any input that will help the team to reach its goals. Don't allow yourself to become angry, get your feelings hurt, or make others feel guilty for not agreeing with your concepts.

"Alex, you seem to disagree with this plan. I could be wrong, but some of your actions and comments lead me to believe you have some concerns. Is that correct?"

This is a calm yet confident way to check it out. You just want him to publicly acknowledge his feelings about the issue. (Come on, Alex! Own it!)

Just like Aggressives, Passive–Aggressives never want to be accountable for their actions.

Addressing the issue leads to two outcomes:

ALEX CAN LIE.

"Oh, I have no problem whatsoever with this plan. It's great."

Fantastic. You can make Alex the head of the committee, ask him to do additional research, or write the report. He will soon learn that displaying passive-aggressive behavior results in extra work. He just wanted to complain without being held accountable for his behavior.

ALEX CAN TELL THE TRUTH.

"Well, as a matter of fact, I think this plan is going to fail for many reasons, including..."

Honesty. You can work with that! But it will be a test of your true character. How do you respond when someone disagrees with you or gives you negative feedback? Many people dive into a big pool of defensiveness.

Instead, invite Alex to prepare a full presentation that explains why your plan is NOT in the best interests of the company, customers, or team members. You may be surprised by his perspective and actually decide to reconsider your strategies. Or...Alex may deeply regret acting like a child and commit to better behavior moving forward.

Did you notice the irony there? No matter what Alex says when confronted, his poor attitude and behavior result in an increased workload. Just to be clear, Passive-Aggressives are definitely not fond of additional work. The lesson for Alex? Speak up and express your opinions instead of hiding behind a childish posture. That doesn't pay off.

> **When people disagree with us RESPECTFULLY in a public forum, how we respond is very important.**

This is one of the hardest times to be assertive, but one of the most necessary. The best assertive response in those cases would be, *"Thank you. I appreciate your willingness to tell me how you feel face-to-face."*

This is the point when most people incredulously scream, *"Are you kidding me?!? I'm supposed to THANK them after all the aggravation they have put me through?"* I get it. Thanking them might sound crazy, but it's the smartest move. We might as well hear what they are thinking about us to our face because they are saying it behind our backs anyway.

Truthfully, those who communicate DISRESPECTFULLY don't deserve our thanks. I'm referring to tactics like yelling, swearing, belittling, or name-calling. Instead, we can let them know that we're willing to meet with them personally (after the public meeting) to discuss the situation in a more professional manner. The fact that they disagree with us isn't a problem. The fact that they express their disagreements in unacceptable or inappropriate ways most certainly is. And you cannot let that go on.

Remember, Passive-Aggressives are at war with us. We can't win unless we know what they're thinking. That's the only way to predict and intercept their next moves.

We have to know how they are feeling if we want to develop a successful strategy to help improve the relationship. Good leaders are excited when their staff members bring contradictory thoughts to the table so they can formulate their plans based on both the pros and the cons of any given situation. Of course, the people with differing opinions need to be "trained" to share those alternative ideas in a mature, professional way. You can set the foundation for that by modeling assertive behavior and reacting in ways that don't meet the Passive-Aggressives' needs. And then what? Most Passive-Aggressives aren't interested in continuing to antagonize someone who will openly and honestly call them out on their behavior.

"Doesn't that seem a little like the passive-aggressive person is winning?"

Consider the bigger picture: both people are losing now. They have lost trust, respect, laughter, and the benefits of a close relationship. The true winner is the one who can stop acting like a child and begin acting like a healthy adult. The true winner is the one who can begin to communicate assertively and lead the way toward a more fulfilling and respectful life. There are no losers in a happy, healthy relationship.

One caveat here. When I talk about being the first person to give in, I'm not referring to abusive, addictive relationships. Giving in and apologizing to hurtful, addictive, or abusive people is going to keep the dysfunctional chain unbroken. Those aren't situations for giving in; they are for getting out.

> **In a non-addictive, non-abusive relationship that becomes characterized by passive-aggressive behaviors, the winner is the one who assertively intervenes and takes action to stop the insanity.**

"What if the Passive-Aggressive lives with me?"

Assuming it's a fairly healthy relationship you want to save and improve (no abuse!), you've got to stop keeping score. Consciously think of nice things you can do for the other person with no expectation of having the favor returned. Be loving, generous, and kind. Do your best to block out the feelings of frustration that have built up. Smile more. Be affectionate. Practice unconditional love for one month. Then, see what happens.

You will probably experience some pleasant moments for a change. It's incredible how quickly the people in your life will respond to your thoughtfulness, tenderness, and openness. You'll start to realize that being assertive feels AMAZING. Avoiding passive-aggressive behavior feels even BETTER.

"That sounds good in theory, but I might need an example."

Now that you have a better understanding of the four different behavior styles, you should be able to predict the potential impact of your communication choices with greater accuracy.

Think cause and effect. If I say this, how will that make the other person feel? Will we both get our needs met? If not, who is on the losing end? What message will each of us be storing in our mental filing cabinets? How will we BOTH feel about the relationship when this conversation or interaction is complete?

Chris and Megan have been married for 12 years. For the most part, they both feel good about each other. The relationship feels relatively balanced and equal.

One weekend, Megan decides she needs to go into the office and get some work done. Chris is upset because Megan is leaving him to entertain the kids, go to the grocery store, stop by the dry cleaners, and help their oldest son with his science fair project. They had originally planned to tackle those items together, but Megan is suddenly out of the picture for the day. How does Chris handle the situation when he feels the score is now Megan-1, Chris-0?

HERE ARE THE OPTIONS:

1. AGGRESSIVE

Using anger or hurt to convince Megan to change her mind and stay home.

Anger: *"Fine, go ahead! I'm tired too, and this is a long list of errands. Can't you get your projects finished before Saturday?*

What's wrong with you? That's just rude! You don't value family time anymore!"

Hurt: *"It's OK, go ahead. One of us should have a productive day; it might as well be you. Since I'm not very good with arts and crafts, I'm pretty sure Bradley will get a bad grade on the science project. But he'll get over it eventually. You go ahead and do what you need to do..."*

2. PASSIVE

Avoiding a conversation about how he really feels or what he wants.

"Sure. It will be quiet at the office, so you can get a lot done. Don't worry about me. I'll make sure everything is finished before you get home. No, really. I'm fine."

(Internal Thoughts)
"I can't believe she's going in to the office today. She knows how much we need to do, and it will take both of us to get everything done. I'm exhausted from a brutal week with clients in town. If she loved me, there's no way she would desert me. It's not fair."

3. PASSIVE-AGGRESSIVE

Avoiding the discussion but vowing to get even.

"Of course. You do that. I'll handle everything here. No problem."

(Internal Thoughts)
"I will not forget about being treated like this. The next time we have something planned, I'm going to conveniently be busy at the last minute. Let's see how she likes that!"

4. ASSERTIVE

Communicating clearly to achieve a win/win solution.

"Megan, I know you've worked hard all week, and so have I. How about this? If you go into the office this morning, I'll hit the grocery store and the dry cleaners while the kids are at their music lessons. Around 2, you could come home and help Bradley with the science project while I go to the gym. We've got the babysitter tonight, so we can both look forward to some alone time later. Would that arrangement work for you?"

The assertive style sounds incredibly sensible and mature, doesn't it? Of course it does. But for some people, this conversation sounds more like a trip through the Twilight Zone. Surreal. Freakish. Pure fiction. It doesn't even seem plausible for couples who primarily communicate using non-assertive styles. But I promise, it is!

> # Choose assertive behavior, and everyone wins.

For those who decide to stick with a non-assertive communication style, the passive-aggressive cycle will keep going. The silent treatment. Traps. Keeping score. Sabotage and subterfuge. And then? They might as well put the marriage counselor and the divorce attorney on speed-dial.

It probably sounds simplistic to say that the whole world needs more assertiveness, but I'm going out on a limb with that statement. You heard it here!

If we could team up to transform all of the angry Passive-Aggressives into rational and predictable people, we could change the world. One person at a time, each Assertive could make a positive impact on the next Non-Assertive.

I know, I know. That's wildly ambitious. Delusional perhaps. But wouldn't that be a great start?

I think we should at least give it a try.

{
REALITY CHECK

Disarm the Passive-Aggressives! Don't give up. Don't give in. Get assertive!

#respectrocks
}

SUMMARY
Action Plan: *Dealing with Passive-Aggressives*

1. Establish a goal to assert yourself, deal with issues head-on, and resolve your conflicts as professionally and maturely as possible.

2. Protect yourself from manipulation by recognizing the signs of passive-aggressive behavior within your relationships. You don't need to be paranoid, but you should pay attention.

3. Analyze your behaviors to determine if your own communication style is fueling the Passive-Aggressives' attacks.

4. Determine if you have done or said anything potentially hurtful (real or perceived) to the Passive-Aggressives in your life. Can you address those issues directly rather than letting them fester?

5. Adopt assertive behavior and use it consistently to disarm Passive-Aggressives when they try to manipulate you through gossip, tattling, silence, or traps.

6. Avoid responding to Passive-Aggressives with the same behavior. End the cycle, and retrain them to treat you with respect by setting a good example.

7. Don't ignore passive-aggressive behavior. You'll only make it worse and encourage more of it. The only time it's beneficial to ignore negative behavior is when people are using the silent treatment to punish you.

But, even then, assertiveness should be the first step.

8. Use assertive behavior at work and at home to transform your relationships, increase your professional success, and improve your overall happiness. ·

9. Remember that there are no winners in relationships with Passives-Aggressives—only losers.

10. Don't give up. Don't give in. Get assertive! That's the ONLY strategy that can improve your relationships and reduce your stress.

What if YOU might be the Passive-Aggressive?

1. Be honest with yourself. Are you holding a grudge against someone? Are you avoiding an honest, direct conversation to resolve the issue but you still want to get revenge? Try to determine the reasons behind those feelings.
2. Start implementing the assertive communication style. Adopt those behaviors, and use constructive responses to discourage others from taking advantage of you in the future.
3. Think in terms of win/win solutions. You deserve to have your needs met, and so do the other people in your life. Can you reframe your relationships to be more collaborative rather than competitive?
4. Stand up for yourself, and set boundaries. You'll minimize the situations that prompt you to seek payback if you don't allow yourself to be mistreated.
5. Don't play games. Say what you mean; mean what you say.
6. Stop using the silent treatment. It's prolonging the misery for everyone. Find the courage to discuss issues or problems in an open, honest way.
7. Resist the urge to keep score in your relationships. Be kind every chance you get, and Karma will be on your side.

8. Be aware of your body language and facial expressions. Make them match your words so others feel confident about understanding your position on the topic at hand.

9. Take responsibility for your actions. No blaming or whining. Accountability will help you begin building your self-esteem.

10. Remember that adopting the assertive style will allow you to improve your relationships and model positive behavior for all of the other people in your life.

chapter
ten

FINAL THOUGHTS

This might be the end of the book, but it's only the beginning of a whole new life for you. It's finally time to launch into your life-long journey of assertive success. And now you know exactly why this is YOUR journey and yours alone, right?

"Because we can't change other people."

Exactly! It's all up to you. You have the choice. You have the control. You have the knowledge. You have the power. And you now have the essential insights (into yourself and others) to understand the instant and enduring impact that healthy communications can have on your life.

> ### The truth is, life would NOT be easier without other people. You just have to CHOOSE the right people. And the right way to communicate.

REMEMBER THIS:

Words have the power to put people down or lift them up.

Hurt them or encourage them.

Accelerate anxiety or provide solace.

Destroy relationships or repair them.

That's some seriously powerful stuff right there.

Purposeful, assertive communication can be a game-changer in every facet of your life. Success. Health. Financial security. Love. Happiness. Quality of life.

You've had a chance to witness firsthand the dysfunction and insanity that comes with the alternatives to the assertive style. And you understand that these options only lead to more manipulation and disrespect, not to mention the disintegration of relationships. They just don't work.

If you want the best possible chances to create healthy, successfully, caring, happy, and productive relationships, you need assertiveness. It's the key to setting fair boundaries, communicating your needs clearly, and demonstrating respect. It can completely transform the way you interact with others.

ASSERTIVENESS
MUST BE THE ANSWER BECAUSE:

- Aggressive behavior means attacking right back.
  Nothing changes.
- Passive behavior means giving in.
  Nothing changes.
- Passive-aggressive behavior means plotting revenge.
  Nothing changes.

"No contest. Assertive behavior is the only real solution."

Well said! That's what I hope you'll remember long after reading this book.

But now that you've acquired this knowledge, it's begging to be used. Think about that. Where would we be today if Leonardo da Vinci got that paint set at his fourth birthday party and just left it in the back of his closet? What a waste! You owe it to yourself to go out and assertively create your own relationship masterpieces.

When you live, breathe, and embrace the principles of assertive communication, amazing things will happen. Just watch for the beautiful changes that will be revealed—even among the most challenging people you deal with every day.

"Sounds incredible. But this isn't going to be easy, is it?"

Nope. It's a tough road. Significant change with positive results never comes easy. You have to WANT things to be different with every fiber of your being. And even more than just wanting it, you have to fight for it.

- Fight for your right to be treated well.
- Fight for your right to be happy.
- Fight for your right to be heard.
- Fight for your right to exist away from toxic people and relationships.

If you don't actively pursue change, everything will stay the same. And "the same" is damaging both your physical health and your mental well-being.

"You're right. I want change, and I'm ready."

I know you are. Deep breath. You have everything you need. You've got the tools, insights, and strategies to transform your relationships with difficult people and enjoy life on a much higher level than you ever imagined.

The success and happiness you truly deserve have been hiding under a giant pile of anger, blame, manipulation, sabotage, and guilt—but you've just uncovered them. And now you can recognize those distractions for what they are: futile attempts to undermine you, manipulate you, and make you feel guilty. Difficult people are doing their best to coerce you into NOT being the person you want to be.

But not anymore. That stops right now!

Choosing assertiveness changes everything. It puts you back in control.

WOW! TAKE THAT IN FOR A MOMENT.

> ### YOU are in charge, and THEY aren't. How powerful is that?

CONGRATULATIONS!

You have your voice back. Your life back. Your sanity back. And as a result, YOU WILL BE HEARD!

It's all up to you now. The future of your relationships is in your hands. I believe in you.

And so the journey begins.

{ REALITY CHECK }

Want to make life easier? Happier? More successful? Choose to be assertive!

#otherswillfollow

ABOUT
CONNIE
PODESTA

Connie Podesta is a game-changing, sales-generating, leadership-developing, revenue-building ball of fire. Her rare blend of laugh-out-loud humor, amazing insights, convention-defying substance and no-nonsense style have made her a consistently in-demand international business speaker for more than 25 years.

Two million people. One thousand organizations. Hall of Fame speaker. Award-winning author. Seven books. Former radio/TV personality. Humanology expert. Licensed professional therapist for 30 years. Executive career, speaking and life coach. Expert on the psychology of sales, leadership, change, communication, and getting your act together! Plus, what we all could probably use in today's crazy world: a comedienne.

BOOK CONNIE
TO SPEAK AT YOUR NEXT EVENT

Connie will dazzle your audience with an unforgettable experience that generates lasting, positive change. She ignites an amazing buzz of energy and empowerment with her high-octane blend of wisdom, humor, and enthusiasm. Best of all, Connie inspires bold action. She challenges her audiences to defy limited thinking and dare to STAND OUT!

CONNIE'S MOST-REQUESTED TOPICS INCLUDE:

- **Lead Like You Mean It!**
  The power of accountability and ownership
- **How to Stand Out from the Crowd: Out-Think, Out-Lead, and Out-Sell the Competition**
  The power of performance and innovation
- **How to Get People on Board**
  The power of consensus and buy-in
- **Selling...Like You've Never Heard It Before**
  The power of persuasion and the psychology of buying behavior
- **Life Would Be Easy if it Weren't for Other People**
  The power of personality and building relationships

CONTACT CONNIE'S TEAM TO CHECK AVAILABILITY
(972) 596-5501 | connie@conniepodesta.com
www.ConniePodesta.com

TOP-RATED BOOKS

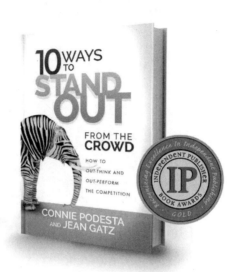

10 WAYS TO STAND OUT FROM THE CROWD

Finally! A business book that isn't boring! Awarded the Independent Publishers award for "most visually stunning business book," Stand Out is an artistic delight chock full of real-life success strategies that can propel the reader to new levels of success—both personally and professionally. TEN condensed books on the TEN hottest topics facing business professionals in today's changing world. Get ready! This may be the first business book that you really just can't put down!

HAPPINESS IS SERIOUS BUSINESS

Happiness doesn't get the respect it deserves. It's rarely seen as a business power trait for increasing results or boosting the bottom line. But fasten your seatbelts! Connie will take you on a wild ride that smashes this perception of happiness and shows you how it can change everything. Your career. Your relationships. Your life. It's a radically different perspective. Packed with striking insights and sprinkled with Connie's irresistible humor, this book documents the extraordinary (and often overlooked) power of happiness. If business success is your goal, it's definitely time to get serious about HAPPINESS.

Winner of the Silver Award from the Nonfiction Book Awards!

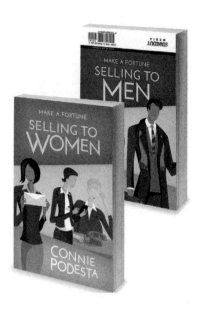

SELLING TO WOMEN / SELLING TO MEN

TWO books for the price of one (back-to-back!). There is no doubt that men and women have very different buying styles. Knowing how to adapt to each gender's preferences is the key to closing more deals and developing long-lasting customers. Discover how to identify gender-specific needs and motivations of potential buyers and then apply that knowledge to powerfully influence their purchase decisions.

TEXTING HARRY

A true story of courage, change, and life's possibilities. Tired and overwhelmed, Harry boarded a flight to Dallas from Boston. He had lost his creative spirit, excitement for new ideas, and passion for adventure. He was ready to give up. Then...he sat down next to Connie. And his life was about to change. The transformation Harry makes in the next few hours is remarkable and poignant. We all know someone like Harry—someone who just needs a reminder that we are never too old to get back on track and experience everything life has to offer. This story will warm your heart and bring a tear to your eye. It's a must-read!

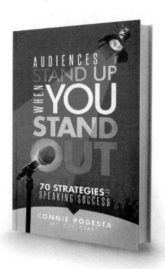

AUDIENCES STAND UP WHEN YOU STAND OUT:
70 Strategies for Speaking Success

Professional speakers are experts at creating the obstacles that hold them back. This book profiles 70 practical things that speakers need to QUIT doing if they're serious about achieving greater success. By applying Connie's proven strategies, speakers can move from earning a good living to establishing themselves as high-profile, high-impact presenters. If you want to take your speaking career to the next level, this is the definitive resource you need!

––––––––––––

All of Connie's products are available for purchase on her website at **ConniePodesta.com.** For details about bulk orders, please call **(972) 596-5501**

CONNECT WITH CONNIE

Phone: **(972) 596-5501**

Email: **connie@conniepodesta.com**

Website: **www.ConniePodesta.com**

Follow Connie:

 Connie Podesta Presents

 Connie Podesta

 @Connie_Podesta

For information about Connie's high-impact retreats for professional speakers, please contact our office:

Connie Podesta Presents, LLC

3308 Preston Road; Suite 350-119

Plano, Texas 75093

INDEX

A

boundaries

    and apologies, 103–04

    establishing, 22, 139, 222

    and passive communicators, 120–22, 136

broken record technique, 100–02

bullying, 26, 70–71, 85–86, 91

C

change

    encouragement to, 30–31

    implementing, 98, 228

    others, 28, 30–31, 225

    yourself, 6, 29, 33, 91–92, 107, 195

child tone, 47

children, 12–13, 43–44, 57–58, 106, 118–20, 131–32, 154–56, 204–05, 208

choice, importance of, 11–12, 38

collaboration, 26, 51–52, 147, 201–02, 209–12, 222

communication, 24–25, 38

    body language, 46–47

    tones, 46–47

    using multiple styles, 126–27

    See also individual communication styles

companies, role of assertive communication in, 42

compromising, 129–30

confidence, 42, 84, 93, 105

    confidence, lack of, 83

conflict, 158–59

confrontations, 2–3, 20, 22, 96–97, 116–17

empathy, 26

entitlement, 60

extroversion and assertiveness, 130–31, 141

F

fairness, 41

fear, 71, 73, 83, 87–88, 102, 116–17, 134

feedback, 24, 29–33, 38, 80, 90–91, 119–20, 152

four communication styles, 24–27, 38

    See also specific communication styles

G

gossip, 113, 170, 178–80, 198–200

guilt, 85, 97, 123–24, 141

    using, 71–74

H

health, 4, 87–88, 116

honesty, 41, 211–12, 222

hurt, and aggressive communication, 71–73, 85, 217

I

"I" vs. "You", 76–78, 85–86

ignoring bad behavior, 32–33, 220

    apropriate times for, 128–29, 207–08

    See also avoidance

intimidation, 26, 67, 70–71, 85–86, 91, 141

introversion and assertiveness, 130–31, 141

intuition, 115–16

    See also passive communication

J

L

M

power, feelings of, 15

professional behavior, and assertiveness, 50–54, 106

psychological rewards, 19–21

pushback, 34–36, 49, 96–99, 105

    See also detours

Q

questions

    about yourself, 6, 59–62

    interactions with aggressive people, 89–90

    on passive-aggressive interactions, 196

    on passive communication, 113

quick fixes, futility of, 5

quitting, 63–64, 106–07

R

reality checks

    assertiveness, 64, 229

    control, 9, 37

    manipulation, 84, 107

    passive-aggressive communicators, 190, 219

    passive communicators, 140, 164

    rewarding bad behavior, 21

relationships

    and assertive communication, 42–43, 55–56, 106

    and passive-aggressive communication, 172–73

    questions about, 61–62

    as source of stress, 1–2

    vs. isolated confrontations, 2–3

Content Development and Editing Services
provided by **Susan Priddy**

Susan Priddy is an award-winning writer and marketing strategist who specializes in targeted business communications that generate real results. Integrating her MBA and Journalism degrees, she is known for developing powerful content infused with strategic focus and creative flair.

www.SusanPriddy.com

Graphic Design and Layout Services
provided by **Kendra Cagle**

Kendra Cagle is an award-winning graphic designer with a Bachelor of Science in Graphic Design from The Art Institute of Fort Lauderdale. She combines creative talents with a passion for art to craft original design for speakers, authors, and fellow entrepreneurs.

www.5LakesDesign.com